FROM the DEPTHS:

A Journey from Addiction, Abuse,

and Homelessness

to Positively Impacting the World

Jimmy Colson

Copyright © Jimmy Colson, 2018
Cover Illustration Copyright © Jimmy Colson, 2018
All Rights Reserved.

http://www.JimmyColson.com
info@JimmyColson.com

Author:
Jimmy Colson

Title:
From the Depths: A Journey from Addiction, Abuse, and Homelessness to Positively Impacting the World

Rights:
All rights reserved. This book or any portion thereof may not be reproduced or used in any manner whatsoever without the express written permission of the author except for the use of brief quotations in a book review.

Printed:
In the United States of America

First Edition:
November 2018

ISBN-13: 978-1-970111-00-2 eBook
ISBN-13: 978-1-970111-01-9 paperback

Imprint:
Published in partnership with Laura Petersen (LaptopLaura.com), Founder of Copy That Pops (CopyThatPops.com).

Dedication

This book is for Joshua, and Liliana, and Sara.
You three are the inner core of the family I always dreamed of
and finally have.
My life is complete.

Table of Contents

Part 1: Introduction 1
This Book Is for You 3
The Real World 5
Disclaimer 6
Family Tree 7

Part 2: Early Family Life 9
Mother 11
Father: "My Pops" - Peter Glen Colson 16
My Birth: November 26, 1972 18
Stepdad 1: "My Dad" - Jack Van Horn 19
My Sister: Melissa (1974) 24
Stepdad 2: Mom's High School Sweetheart - Jim 28
My Brother: Eli (1979) 32
Babysitters and Abuse 33

Part 3: Family & Foster Care Roller Coaster 37
Loaded Guns to Foster Care 39
One Summer in Heaven 41
My Pops Takes Me Away, For a While 42
Boyfriend 1: The Man-Child - Gary 48
Mom Goes to Jail 51
A Second Vision for a Better Future 54
Seeds of Entrepreneurism 58
Sister Pays the Price for Taking Us In 59
Boyfriend 2: Limp Dick Prick - James 67

Part 4: Teenage Tribulations 77
13 Years Old: With a Gang 79
14 Years Old: On the Street and Suicidal 81

Melissa Gets Caught Selling Drugs ... 83
Mortifying School Assembly ... 86
Hit by Pizza Driver + CPS ... 89
The Boys Home + Running Away ... 91
Las Vegas ... 101
Becoming One of the Bad Guys I Despised ... 103
CYA + Escaping to Las Vegas ... 108
Gma Surprisingly Takes Us In ... 114
More Mistakes, Time to Fly ... 123
16 Years Old: On My Own ... 133
17 Years Old: Leaving Las Vegas ... 136
Hawaii ... 141

Part 5: Becoming an Adult ... 147
18th Birthday Trauma ... 149
Back to Las Vegas ... 151
Mean Streets ... 157
Rough Life and More Fights ... 165
Katie + Sacramento ... 176
Back to Las Vegas + Baby Joshua ... 182
Monkey in the Back ... 187
Losing Everything ... 190
A Second Chance to Be a Better Man ... 194
On Again, Off Again ... 196
Family Drama + Marriage Crumbling ... 199
Bad Decision: Acid for the Second Time ... 202
The Divorce Finalized ... 204
Terrible Car Accident ... 209
Crazy Times ... 213

Part 6: The Spark of Change ... 221
Realizing the Codependent Addiction ... 223
Self-Discovery + More Family Drama ... 227

Tina ... 233
My First Taste of Prosthetics and Orthotics ... 235
Best Friend Tony ... 240
The Worst Night of My Life ... 245
Opened an Office But Wanted More ... 252
The Beginning of My Company ... 254
White Supremacists on PCP ... 257
Business Growth + Partying Too Hard ... 260
Sara ... 265
Losing My Dad + Sara ... 276
True Rock Bottom ... 278

Part 7: Transformation ... 281
Growth and Winning Sara Back ... 283
World Travel Opens Your Eyes ... 286
Cremating My Mom ... 295
Death of My Biological Father ... 299
Path for Good Is Finally Clear ... 300
Positive Recognition ... 303
A Call to Positive Action ... 305

Part 8: Lessons Learned ... 309
Life Lessons ... 311
Princess Liliana ... 317
Reef Tanks: A Healthy Addiction ... 322
The Next Chapter ... 332
A Final Note to My Family ... 333
A Final Note to You ... 335

About the Author ... 342

Want More? ... 345

PART 1

INTRODUCTION

This Book Is for You

I awoke this morning thinking back to the many struggles my family has endured throughout our lives.

If you met me as I am today, you would not believe it all.

Sure, now I am an American Board Certified Orthotist who has been recognized by Congress for humanitarian work that my wife and I have done within our community. I have had my reef tanks featured on a TV show on *Animal Planet*. And I am also the CEO of a multi-million dollar company.

But the path here was long, hard, and uncertain.

What I am about to tell you is all true. These are my memoirs of sorts. Some of the names and details have been changed. But the rest? It's too crazy to have been made up.

A lot of what I share here I am not proud of — I made a lot of mistakes.

I was all the way under, in the dark depths. But by putting it all out for you to see, for the world to see, I believe that I can help others.

My big dream is to help change the world for the better, one person at a time.

If you 'get me' in these stories — if you have gone through or are going through similar things — then know that this book is for you.

You are not alone. You are loved. You *can* take control of your destiny. You have a voice, so let it be heard.

Even when you feel there is no way up, keep going. And keep growing.

Life is full of abundance and opportunity if you push through and keep your eyes open.

It may be difficult, but the journey is worth it.

And I am here cheering you on, knowing what you have gone through and believing in you all the same.

Now, let's flash back to the times before I took control of my life…

Jimmy Colson
Las Vegas, Nevada
August, 2018

Jimmy Colson

The Real World

We went without food all the time.

We used to wash ourselves in friends' sinks or gas station restrooms because we had no running water.

We would light candles because we had no electricity for weeks at a time.

We had to go to the bathroom outside. So we would dig holes.

We endured so many struggles.

That's what happens when you were born in the 1970s to a hippy chick mom and a string of men that she wanted you to call 'Daddy.'

Disclaimer:
The events and conversations in this book have been set down to the best of the author's ability, although some names and details have been changed to protect the privacy of individuals.

Content Warning:
This book contains some adult material and language including stories about or references to child abuse, drug abuse, sexual abuse, rape, suicide, depression, racism, and physical violence.

Jimmy Colson

Family Tree

Helpful diagram for your reference.

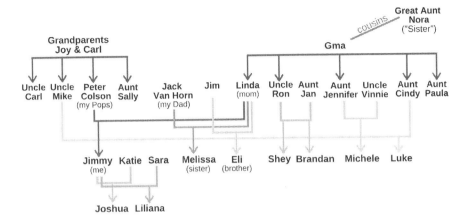

PART 2
EARLY FAMILY LIFE

MOTHER

My Mother's Childhood

My grandmother — my "Gma" — was an alcoholic who left three of her five children (my mother, my Uncle Ron, and my Aunt Paula) on my great-aunt's doorstep and never took custody of them again.

After that, she would pick and choose when to jump in and out of my mother's life.

Drunk most of the time, my Gma made sure to leave an impression on everyone she met. Most times that impression was very bad.

She constantly threw hurtful insults and called my mother a whore even though she was still as pure as snow.

She gave my mother used lipstick as a Christmas gift.

Up and Down

Despite a rough start in life, my mother was a beautiful woman with bright grayish-blue eyes, long blond hair, a sultry smile, and a big heart with tons of charisma.

Men flocked to her. She could have whoever she wanted. My mother could always draw a whistle — or a crowd — when she walked on by.

But in addition to her good looks and charm, she was somewhat of a disturbed woman with abandonment issues.

The eldest of five children, my mother was devastated at being discarded at a very young age.

My mother resented everyone she was close to for this reason. Her pain was hers and hers alone.

She always wondered why she was not chosen to stay with her mother.

- "Why was I, the eldest, tossed away to another family?"
- "Does Mommy not love me?"
- "Am I not pretty enough?"
- "Am I not smart enough?"
- "What could I have possibly done wrong?"

These questions haunted my mother until her final lost and lonely days.

I believe that she could never rid herself of her demons or her feelings of inadequacy. Why would Gma have so many children and then just give three of them away?

My mother had so many complexes. She suffered from manic depression (or bipolar disorder), had an addictive personality, and was one of the biggest hypochondriacs you could ever meet.

She would get a splinter and act as if she were going to lose her arm.

But I loved her.

I loved her more than the moon and stars. She was such a beautiful, lost soul. I believed when we looked into one another's eyes, we could see each other's essence. I could gaze into her soul and see the pureness that was never fully able to manifest. It was never nurtured.

She never stood a chance.

No 'I love you' or kisses good night. It was tough being abandoned. It was tough being unwanted and unloved. It was unfair.

Life was unfair.

Sister and Her Mother

When my Gma abandoned three of her kids, there was a kind-hearted older lady and her mother who took them in and tried their best. This lady, a great-aunt we called "Sister," and her mother were like saints.

They worked hard in a laundromat, trying to give the children a better life. They did the best they could and sacrificed their lives to make a better place for the three abandoned innocents left on their front doorstep.

And they never asked for much. The love of the children was the payment they desired, but never quite received.

They spoiled these kids with what little they had. They were hard-working, lower class people who loved, cared for, and tried to protect the children.

They tried their best, but this was the late 60s, and our country was at war.

A Country at War

Sirens blazed, music blasted, and the world changed right before everyone's eyes.

Our country was filled with drugs, propaganda, and people fighting "the Man," fighting the system.

Peace signs flashed, while loved ones came home in body bags. Mind-altering substances were mainstream and mainlined. Psychedelics were passed around like candy.

Half the country was lost in a dream world, while the other half was fighting an unwinnable war.

Why were we sending our children to the other side of the world to be slaughtered?

Half were being shot at, killed, and forced to do horrible things to survive. The other half back home screamed for peace and love.

And for all, the scars were not only on their bodies but also deep within their souls.

Our whole country was in an uproar.

Times were changing, and so was the world around my mother.

Mom at 16

My mother left home at 16 years old to be married to her first husband.

He was a chubby Hispanic gentleman who loved her, but they had nothing in common. She used the marriage as a way to run away. It was an attempt to escape feeling unloved.

But how can you run away from yourself?

You can never outrun your own demons. They haunt you. They grow to hold you down. They can take over your mind, body, and soul.

Demons do not disappear; they lay dormant until the time is right. Then they take hold and engulf you. The demons want nothing more than to watch you fail.

You have to find something positive to focus on, or they will pull you under. They pulled my mother under.

FATHER: "MY POPS" - PETER GLEN COLSON

"My Pops"

Mom's first marriage was short-lived, and she soon met my biological father. A short, stocky man with kaleidoscope eyes, an infectious laugh, and a zest for doing crazy things.

His name was Peter Glen Colson. I call him "my Pops."

My Pops was a year younger than my mother and was known to have a couple of screws loose. He believed he was from the planet Mars and, by his actions, you might have believed him.

He was one of four children. He had two brothers (one of them named Mike, who you will hear about later) and a sister.

His mother was very loving, and his father was very abusive. He told me of the unimaginable beatings he took at his father's hands.

He had a unique charisma that drew people to him.

His laugh still rings in my ears.

But he was definitely a wild man. He was a loose cannon who could spout off at any time. He was untamed and incorrigible, a man-child, my father.

While his mental problems were not yet fully seen, they were growing within him. They were taking hold and would soon own him. He was not yet consumed by the imaginary life that I will share with you later in this journey.

Mom and My Pops

Two broken people — two lost souls — harboring resentment toward the entire world. Rebelling, reaching out, and putting a middle finger up to all authority figures. Nobody would tell them what to do. They controlled their own destinies.

My father would steal police cars just for kicks. He would ride his Harley Davidson like his hair was on fire and he was on the 'Highway to Hell.'

He was a mystery to her. He was someone she could not figure out or understand. He was her escape from the world. He was her wild man, and she was his muse.

She could be the Bonnie to his Clyde. They could scorch the world. Set it on fire.

But that grows old all too quickly. He became nothing more than her stepping stone.

His mental issues were bubbling to the light, and her insecurities were way too much of a burden to overcome. They were lost children having a child.

My mother decided to leave my Paranoid Schizophrenic father for their next door neighbor while she was pregnant with me.

MY BIRTH: NOVEMBER 26, 1972

Hello, World

My mother gave birth to me on her 19th birthday in Pasadena, California. That year, November 26 also happened to be Thanksgiving. So, on this day, I decided to join the party. It was my first, but surely not my last.

Fun Fact:
This book debuted for its bestseller launch 46 years later on November 26, 2018. It hit #1 in four categories, and I am forever grateful to all who supported me.

STEPDAD 1: "MY DAD" - JACK VAN HORN

"My Dad"

My new stepfather was the first person I would call "Daddy." And he is who I refer to as "my dad" to this day. His name was John Raymond Van Horn. He also went by Jack.

He is the man who would help me become a man — the person I would learn morals, sports, manners, and such. He was a good man. He also had far too many demons.

When he met my mother, he was married to his high school sweetheart. They had a little girl, his princess. But he turned his back on both of them to appease my mom.

He left the family he had moved from New Jersey to California to make a life with my mom: his new muse.

They had a whirlwind love affair.

It happened behind my father's and Jack's wife's backs.

They were all living in an age of free love and free-flowing drugs.

My Dad's Family

My dad was raised by his multi-millionaire adoptive family. They always wanted the best for him, as they never had a biological son of their own.

He also had an adoptive sister to whom he was very cruel. I remember his telling me a story of when she wanted to climb up to his treehouse with him. He dropped a hammer on her head.

He had a disconnect and did not want to be loved.

He could not, and would not, allow anyone in. No one was allowed to love him since he had no love for himself.

He always resented his adoptive parents because "they were not his real parents." He believed that they could not possibly love him since his birth parents did not.

Left for adoption at a very young age, my dad was always waiting for more abandonment.

It became a self-fulfilling prophecy.

If he could push away the world, no one could abandon him again.

His biological sister was a thorn in his side. She was also adopted, but took the high road and believed that she was blessed. She lived an amazing life. And my dad never understood how she could believe in the love she received. That was one of the biggest divides in their relationship.

My dad's family made most of their money in landfills in Florida, real estate in New Jersey, and also in the stock market. They were self-made millionaires living the American Dream.

They wanted to share their wealth with their children.

Jack's sister took to this lifestyle and thrived. But my dad would have nothing of it. This was not the life he chose.

He wanted to lead his own life.

He wanted to be as far away from them as he could.

So, after my dad graduated from high school, he immediately joined the Navy to become a boatswain's mate. That way he did not need to live the life his family wanted for him. He never wanted to run the family business or go to college.

He would make a life for himself.

Enter: My Mother

My dad (my stepfather) was much more stable than my Pops (my biological father).

My dad had a good head on his shoulders and a great smile. He was a poet and very deep in his thoughts. He was smart and talented.

His long locks flowed, and he looked very much like the Jesus mural on our wall.

He was what my mother was looking for:
• A father for me.
• A man who could love her son unconditionally.

My dad's family was very disappointed in him though. He left his high school sweetheart wife for some Jezebel with a nice smile. He abandoned his daughter Diane, the apple of his eye, to raise me, a little bastard child.

To them, my mother was an abomination. She was a product of a new age, a Baby Boomer having a baby.

She was destruction. She ruined their son's life. They decided that we were all below them.

We were all unworthy of their name, love, and all that came with it. We were pretty much exiled.

We were the damned.

A Rough Start to an Even Rougher Childhood

And I? I navigated the world nameless, in a sense. I was technically a Colson, not a Van Horn, not one of them.

I was a child who was loved, hated, lost, and yet somehow found.

I was a product of what times were like in the early 1970s, growing up with parents who were a part of a generation that changed family values and made 'free love' their battle cry.

And I was nameless for a reason. My dad wanted to adopt me and give me the Van Horn name. I even went by "Jimmy Van Horn" in school whenever I could.

But my mom wouldn't allow my last name to be changed because she would lose the Welfare benefits. I was a child in the system. I was a paycheck and free food stamps.

I was a blessing and a curse.

I was a reminder of my crazy fly-by-the-seat-of-his-pants biological father. I had Peter's eyes. Blue as the ocean with the specs of crazy all rolled into one.

A couple of years into my mom's and Jack's relationship? More dysfunction.

Drugs, parties, séances, and abuse were all happening. I was told by other family members of the séances and orgies. I was told of snorting, injecting, popping pills, and trying to function as rational adults.

And when did my mother's addiction truly start? I will never know the full truth.

Was she on drugs since I was born? Did it start not too long after?

I wish she were alive today to answer some of my questions. I wish I could go back to before many of her drug-induced strokes messed with her mind.

I wish, I wish, I wish — but these wishes will never come true.

I ask my uncle and my aunts a lot. They fill me in on little bits and pieces, but I can never get the full picture. Maybe I will never know.

MY SISTER: MELISSA (1974)

Melissa is Born

Two years of being an only child were soon to come to an end.

On a cold winter day in 1974: poof, I became a brother.

Melissa was a little red-skinned, black-haired baby girl. She was beautiful; she was mine. It was time for me to grow up at all of two years old.

They called me "the little man."

I was the one who comforted my mom when she broke down, cuddled with my dad until he passed out on the couch, and cradled my baby sister until she fell asleep.

The Calm Before the Storm

As far as I knew, life was great.

Heck, you might have thrown a white picket fence in the front yard and made a Norman Rockwell painting out of us. But looks can be very deceiving.

In 1976, my sister was all of two years old, and I was four going on 20. I was quiet, introspective, and a bit of a loner. You could give me a toy, and I would be lost in it for hours.

My sister, on the other hand, ran the house. She crawled and walked around saying, "Me Issa, Me Issa."

She had become a terror.

I remember once my dad woke up with a shredded hundred dollar bill on his face. Melissa had gotten into his wallet and tore apart all of his bills.

She was hell on wheels, the destroyer of my toys, and the taker of my parents' hearts.

I had to figure out how to control this little hellion. I had to figure out what made her tick. She was the Energizer Bunny long before he existed.

She was my opposite — the Yin to my Yang.

There were good times too though.

I remember dancing with my mother and Melissa to *Gypsy* by Fleetwood Mac all the time. We would spin and swirl away.

When I hear this song now, I look back at my mom as our gypsy: "A memory is all that is left of her now."

And back then, my sister was still mine.

She was my "Me Issa."

But at this young age, it was the beginning of a tough journey for both of us. We had no idea that foster care, boys and girls homes, incarceration, and being forgotten were in our futures.

We were innocence lost.

We were balls and chains to free love. We were becoming the enemy.

We were the product of Baby Boomers having children while they were not much more than children themselves. Melissa's father (my dad) seemed like a good man to me. He always showed me love, as if I were his own.

My dad was the first to introduce me to sports. He sat me down and had me pick the teams on his football bets. He taught me how to choose, and I even helped him win on my first try.

And he gave me two choices of football teams to support. He said I could choose either the Pittsburgh Steelers or the New York Giants (he was from New Jersey) and I had to stay a fan for the rest of my life.

This was the start of my learning loyalty.

I chose the Steelers and became a diehard fan.

I also noticed the number 11 on one of his sports cards and became fascinated by it. Every time the clock would read 11:11 I would make a wish. I continue to do that to this very day.

I loved watching the games and felt these were our best times together. These were some of the best moments in childhood for me.

My dad would cheer on the Steelers and so would I. It was our bonding. These times helped mold me into the man I am today.

I had no idea then, but this was the beginning of the end of our happy little family.

Skeletons in the Closet

This man was my dad in every sense of the word. But behind closed doors, he was very abusive. He struck my mom and sexually abused her.

She kept her chin up and hid it from us children.

Suicide was an option my mother considered her whole life. She talked about it since she was very young. She dreamt of the day she could shed herself of her demons.

She did not want to live but was much too scared to die.

She was our protector and our curse.

She was everything we needed and all that was bad in society. She was our Mommy.

My mother had the kindest of hearts that, once the drugs masked her pain, would soon turn as black as the tar she injected into her arms.

We were truly happy children, but looks are very deceiving.

This life had skeletons in the closet. It had lies, deceit, and so much pain that would all bubble to the surface in 1977.

STEPDAD 2: MOM'S HIGH SCHOOL SWEETHEART - JIM

Mom's Downward Spiral

My mother would often disappear. She would be gone a day here, a day there, or just a couple of hours at a time.

Why?

It turns out that she was "helping" a friend of hers from high school. He had returned from Vietnam with shrapnel littered throughout his body. He was scarred both physically and mentally.

Do you see the pattern? It had already started.

From one man to another, to another, to yet another: this was a never-ending pattern. My mother was like a revolving door when it came to relationships.

She was codependent before she even knew what it meant.

Her relationships never completely ended either. She would always end up back with a previous lover when she became single once again. That is if she even waited in between relationships. She always had another man lined up.

My poor mother never knew what it was like to be alone. She never learned how to think for herself. She never gained inner peace. She never learned how to love herself, and so I believe she never truly learned to love anyone else wholeheartedly.

Lost in love over and over, she could never find herself. She was a dreamer, a poet, a lover, a codependent, a druggy, a wife, a cheater, an absent parent, and our Mommy.

We would often ask my stepfather, "Where is Mommy?"

He got angry and became more abusive towards her. Now we could start to see the other side — glimpses of anger, hate, and frustration. He had had enough. Knowing the kind of woman my mother was, he knew he was becoming a part of the past.

When my mother decided to pack up everything in the house, I remember crying my eyes out. "Why are we leaving?"

My stepfather Jack was my hero. Despite his flaws, he loved us (and I did not know that he hit my mom until later as an adult). A poor mouse could not have even found a crumb on the ground when my mother was done packing up all of our belongings. The house was left barren.

Heartbroken and alone, my dad lost all he had built in one fell swoop. We were gone.

This was the beginning of the end of our so-called happy little family. And I believe this is what sent my stepfather into a spiral that would drive him to live on the streets for over a decade.

I was lost too, and this is when things began to get out of control.

This is when the wheels fell off.

No more white picket fences or happy endings.

Enter: Jim

My mother moved us into the home of (and eventually married) the man for whom she left my stepfather. This man was Jim, her high school sweetheart.

He is the person I was named after (a fact I did not know until I was an adult) and also the man I despised most in life.

Jim's mind was still lost back in Vietnam. He was handsome and had a bad boy streak that my mother always looked for in her men.

I remember Jim mumbling to himself on many occasions. He had psychological issues that would soon be seen not just by me, but by everyone.

If my stepfather Jack would buy me a stuffed animal, Jim would buy me the same type, only bigger. He bought Melissa and me everything we could ever want at Christmas. He bought me every Star Wars figure that came out. Opening those boxes were the highlights of any Christmas, but it always brought me back to thinking of my dad.

Even at an early age, I knew love is not something you can purchase. Love comes from within one's heart. These actions did not come from his heart. So, I began to resent him.

I missed the life we used to have and wanted no part in this new one. Maybe I could have tried harder, but I was a child who missed his dad.

I was lost and alone. And Jim was cruel.

He used to ask me to bring him the toilet and laugh at me when I would try to rip it out of the bathroom floor. I was so young that I took his impossible request literally.

Jim would do disgusting things too like flatulating in our faces or telling us to pull his finger. His stench still haunts me to this very day. I can hear his haunting laugh as I write this.

He had Lupus. He had demons. He had become a demon in my eyes. I am not sure if he was always evil, but that is what I saw. He was pure evil to me.

He was a syringe, he was a line, he was a pill.

He was a party, he was an orgy, he was the bane of my existence.

He became my mother's addiction.

He was my enemy. I remember his hitting my mother in front of my sister and me. She would scream for us to get away and go into the other room.

I tried to smash my peanut butter and jelly sandwich in his face once. My mother took the abuse twice as hard. I tried to protect her but ended up doing more harm than good.

You could see the hate build between Jim and me.

Jim cruelly called my mom "Eagle Beak" because of her pronounced nose. He loved her, he hated her, and he decided to have a child with her. It's 1979 and winter time again.

Snow is on the ground in the High Desert of California, and I would soon receive a new blessing.

MY BROTHER: ELI (1979)

Eli Arrives

My little brother Eli was born in January of 1979. I was excited to have someone more like me. Someone to teach how to play ball and ride a bike. Someone to have fun with. And I hoped that he would be the opposite of my little sister.

Eli was my everything.

All I wanted in this world was to protect my siblings, both of them. They were mine. I was the one who would show them right from wrong. I would never let anyone hurt them. I thought that I could shelter them from the abuse.

But I was a child, I was naïve, and I was completely wrong.

BABYSITTERS AND ABUSE

Neglected

We three children were left with a string of terrible babysitters, and I have a lot of haunting memories from this.

I remember Eli painting the walls and his crib with poop because they left him in unchanged diapers for hours.

I remember we were left alone for long periods of time and hearing my brother's never-ending cries from his crib.

Some memories haunt you much more than the others do.

Something Far Worse

There is one memory that I still cannot let go of. I was seven years old, and Melissa was five. A despicable man in his mid-20s, who lived down the street from us, was babysitting. He was supposed to watch out for us.

Instead, he grabbed Melissa, slammed the door behind him, and sexually abused her.

I could not protect my little sister. I could not stop this grown man from shutting the door and keeping it locked shut. I could not stop my sister's screams in pain.

She yelled my name, begging for my help.

She cried and cried. She screamed at me through the locked door to help her escape this evil predator. I tried to force the door open, I tried running into it, but it didn't budge.

I was defeated, I was lost, I was no longer a child. I was a scared young man at all of seven years old.

Such a young age and I had already seen things no child ever should — physical, mental, and sexual abuse.

I shed a few tears for my sister while writing this and how she lost her innocence. Nearly 40 years later, and I still feel the loss. We both lost our innocence on that horrible day. I lost a little, but my sister lost so much more.

Melissa was robbed of her childhood.

She had always been so spunky and full of life. But, after that, Melissa went from being a hellion to a hurt, lost, little girl.

Why didn't her new step daddy Jim protect her?

Why couldn't her big brother Jimmy protect her?

Sadly, this isn't the only case of sexual abuse I know about in our family.

Jim's brother Frank, after discovering that someone molested his friend's daughter, went and killed the girl's parents because they were aware of what was going on. He justified killing the parents because they knew about the horrible abuse and did nothing to protect the little girl.

Frank was sentenced to life in prison, but he was just released a few weeks ago (as I write this part of my story in August 2018) from prison after serving close to 40 years.

I sometimes think about if I were in Frank's position.

What would I do if anyone tried to harm either of my children?

What would I have done back when Melissa's life was shattered, had I been older, bigger, and stronger?

I know I would have served a life sentence for what I would do. I know that would bring out the crazy that has been repressed deep inside me for a very long time.

This is the side of me that I never want to see again.

PART 3

FAMILY AND FOSTER CARE ROLLER COASTER

Jimmy Colson

LOADED GUNS TO FOSTER CARE

Guns

Jim left loaded guns laying around and talked about Vietnam all of the time. Guns were everywhere. You could trip over a rifle just walking on by to grab a snack from the kitchen.

One morning, Melissa got ahold of one of these rifles and pulled the trigger. It blew a hole in the wall just a few inches away from my head. My ears rang and my head throbbed terribly. I cried uncontrollably. I was two inches from dying much too early.

Mom Gives Up

Not too long after this, my mother started threatening suicide on a regular basis. She was defeated by the needle, by Jim's fists, by her love, her enemy, her husband.

For her first attempt at suicide, my mother decided to slice her wrists. Her strength was gone, as was her mind. She had given up on life. What she did not realize was she had also given up on us, her children. This started the spiral of terrible events that would last throughout most of our childhoods.

Still, we idolized our mom.

For every strength she possessed, she also had a severe weakness. For every kindness she shared, she had a dark side. My mother was now well on her path to mental facilities, drug rehabilitation centers, and even regular incarceration.

Thrown into "The System"

With my mother unable to properly care for us, I was taken into the child welfare system. I was still the unwanted.

The first time I was taken away, Melissa and Eli stayed with Jim. I was seen as the bastard. Jim was happy to have me gone. I felt unloved and abandoned.

At this time in life, I was now old enough to see what was real. I became the enemy. I became a child thrust fully into the system.

We all were before long.

"If we weren't getting this money, we wouldn't even have you!" In my experience, most foster families were cruel. We were just paychecks for them.

So, this became life.

I was tossed in and out of foster homes until my Aunt Jennifer, Uncle Vinnie, and little cousin Michele sprung me out.

ONE SUMMER IN HEAVEN

Hope

The one summer that I lived with aunt, uncle, and cousin was one of the best of my entire childhood. I could be a kid again. I went to boys clubs, not boys homes.

Those days were like heaven on Earth for me.

Aunt Jennifer and Uncle Vinnie treated me very well. I felt wanted and loved.

I had fun playing video games like a normal kid.

I had no worries in the world.

I enjoyed that short time in life more than I can express in these pages.

The boys club that I got to join taught me so much. I learned to play chess, pool, Stratego (a fun strategy board game), and so much more. Those days gave a child like me hope.

Hope is a powerful tool to give someone.

With hope, you can move mountains and believe in your dreams. I knew then that I deserved more, wanted more, and would find a way to accomplish more…someday.

MY POPS TAKES ME AWAY, FOR A WHILE

Pulled Away

That incredible summer of 1980 was cut short when my biological father decided to take me away.

At seven years old, I was just entering the first grade after being held back in Kindergarten because I was diagnosed with dyslexia (I was lucky that my teacher caught it at such a young age).

My Pops pulled me out of a wonderful environment full of stability for something terrible.

He was my biological father, he argued, and he wanted to "teach me how to become a Colson."

I was now living with this man I had barely known since I was very young. He was a stranger. And he was a Schizophrenic. His reason, common sense, and compassion had left him a long time ago.

I do believe he loved me in the only way he knew how. But this was about to be one crazy ride.

Insanity

As a child himself, my Pops and his siblings had it tough. They took savage beatings at their father's hands.

(Both of my biological grandfathers died before I could even form a clear memory of them, so I only know about this from stories.)

Maybe this contributed to my Pops' mental decay. He made *One Flew Over the Cuckoo's Nest* seem like a tame fairytale.

He believed we were from the planet Mars and had computers for brains. He also told me that I had thousands of brothers and sisters who were created when the telephone poles pulled semen from him to impregnate all of the women in town.

Wow. At that age, I believed I had a huge family.

He had a girlfriend who was a nurse during this time. We lived in a nice house in Orange County, California and outwardly looked like we lead a normal life like most.

But he told me stories about how we were different from others and that we had a higher calling.

He worshipped pyramids and the moon and always included one of each object whenever he signed his name.

He told me that my initials were J. C., not only because my legal name was Jimmy Colson but also because I was Jesus Christ. He added the weight of the world onto my tiny shoulders. He said that I had to live the life he was going to teach me.

He confused me, he tormented me, and he took what little bit of a childhood I had left and made it a blur.

This was a nightmare that I did not know how to escape.

Was this better than the foster homes? Was I coming or was I going? What was my purpose in life? So many questions filled my head.

My Pops did not believe in toys. He told me, "You are a young man and need to be *a man*." No ifs-ands-or-buts about it. So, as Christmas presents, I got socks, pajamas, and Playboy magazines.

Can you imagine just turning eight and not getting a single toy for Christmas? I unwrapped Playboys instead. Soon, I was given X-rated magazines full of intercourse too.

All of eight years old and I was expected to know a woman's intimate body parts. My Pops wanted me to explain in detail what each part was and what I was supposed to do with it sexually.

I was mortified, lost, and hurt. I was a child who had so much inappropriate pressure put on my shoulders.

"I was supposed to do what with her what?"

He built me a treehouse where I was forced to store this collection of horrors he bestowed upon me. Instead of being a fun, safe place for a kid to escape from the cruel world, this treehouse had to be packed full of naked women I was supposed to "know what to do with."

Crueler still, my Pops would ask me if I was still a virgin. When I would reply, "Yes," he would chime in with, "You are not a Colson. You are not my son!"

I was lost and destroyed.

I was still a nameless bastard, even to my own father.

How could I, Jesus Christ (as he called me), have to endure such criticism, such ridicule, such shame?

School

With all the insanity at home, I lost myself in my school work. I had (and still have) a love for numbers. I also enjoyed reading and writing, but mathematics was my favorite. I was even featured with two other children in the newspaper doing 10-digit by 10-digit multiples in the first and second grades.

I could figure out equations. They made me happy. Math was my escape.

Numbers do not lie. Numbers do not hurt you. Numbers were and always will be my salvation. When I was diagnosed with dyslexia, that put an even bigger fire under me. I knew what I was reading, but when I tried to write words down, my 'b' would end up as a 'd.'

In so many different ways, my mind had a disconnect. I knew what was correct. It all just got lost in translation traveling from my head to my hand.

I am very lucky that they caught my dyslexia early.

Fun Escapes

I was also diagnosed with asthma, so I started running and riding my bike everywhere.

My Pops and I put together a Schwinn bicycle from scratch. It was a project that was meant for bonding between us.

I loved my bike, and I rode it everywhere. I put my baseball cards in the spokes to make it sound like his Harley Davidson.

The bicycle also had a big spotlight on the front that turned on as the tires moved.

It was my other escape.

I would ride it for hours. I pretended it was my Harley. With it, I could travel anywhere my imagination could take me.

This was the first time I actually felt close to my Pops.

That was until I rode my bike to the grocery store one day and watched it get stolen, right in front of my eyes. I chased the kid out of the parking lot. But he was much faster, and there went my escape from the cruel world.

My Pops also taught me how to weld.

We welded a metal spaceship that I sketched out from memory. It looked like the ship we had seen in Battlestar Galactica.

It was great.

Some of my friends felt bad for my never having any toys and would give me a few of theirs. I then swapped them for other toys: "Hey, I will trade you this Army man for your Star Wars figure."

I realized that if I wanted something badly enough, I would have to go and get it.

It was me against the world. Throw me adversity, and I would own it.

I was already a survivor at an incredibly young age. I promised myself then that I was above my living conditions. I would not be a product of what I had seen or experienced and would be a difference maker.

I would make my own way.

I did not have a path yet, but when one presented itself, I would know it and make it mine.

I wanted to save the world. I just did not know how yet.

Mom Is Back

Around this time — I was still about eight years old — my mother decided to get back on her feet and wanted her children back.

Jim took Eli, and I would not see him again for a couple more years.

Melissa was already back and living with our mom.

I thought we were piecing our family back together. Maybe a couple of years, some super glue, and some duct tape could make everything better. We could erase our pain, or at least mask it.

This could be a new beginning. This could get us back on track as a family.

Boy, was I ever wrong!

BOYFRIEND 1: THE MAN-CHILD - GARY

Mom's Boyfriend

Our mother had met another man (or, I should say, man-child) named Gary. His family had money, and he was a trust fund junky. We were told not to ask any questions about where the money came from (it was real estate and possibly old Mafia money).

Despite the free flow of cash for Gary, we all lived in a little shack next door to City Hall in Lancaster, California. They called this shack "the Dungeon." It was a faded green color. Imagine baby food peas as paint.

This shack was old, dingy, and a hang out for all the local drug addicts. It should have been demolished. Gary's parents owned it, along with other real estate properties all around town.

This was now life.

Drugs were done in front of us all the time: syringes blazed, arms were tied off, people passed out half overdosed.

We had to hear our mother scream out during sex every night too. Her yelling, "Oh, Bebe! Oh, Bebe!" still haunts me. My sister and I were so disgusted that we often covered our heads with pillows and cried ourselves to sleep at night.

This was truly worse than any hell I could imagine.

I remember Gary would put a pair of pliers on his tighty-whitey underwear and start screaming as if he caught his penis in the pliers: "Help, help, Mr. Bill! Mr. Bill, my penis is stuck!"

I think he got 'Mr. Bill' from a Saturday Night Live video, but I'm still not sure why he did what he did.

He was another in a long line of mentally unstable and unqualified father figures my mother presented to us, for us. This was a disturbed man-child with Crabs that ran all up through his ample chest hair, who lived life the way he wanted.

He wasn't physically abusive to our mom, which was different from her other relationships, but he threatened me a few times and kicked me hard in the ribs even though I was just a kid.

He was a bully.

He wanted me to treat him as a father.

I wanted nothing to do with him.

He repulsed me.

His very being made my stomach curl.

The Hell Worsens Still

My mom used to clean different men's houses naked to make money for more drugs. They made my little sister and me watch pornography as our mom cleaned.

One man stood out. His name was Dallas.

Dallas was an older man in his mid-50s with a pot belly and is the most disgusting person I remember from childhood. While making us watch pornography, he would wear a cowboy hat and nothing more. He would sit there and masturbate in front of us. I remember one video in particular called *The Talking Vagina*.

It was horrible; it was our life.

This was beyond unfair to us children. I was destroyed, as was Melissa.

I could no longer look into our mother's eyes and see her soul. Our mother was hollow. She was a shell of who I knew she could be. She was defeated. She had given up.

Our mother only cared about where her next fix was coming from. The desire for the drugs grew, and so did the group of friends Gary and she ran with.

MOM GOES TO JAIL

Back and Forth

When I was about 10 years old, our mom was incarcerated for the first time for drug possession and theft.

Melissa and I were thrust back into the system, into foster homes, and into a life separated from our family.

Luckily, Jack was able to get my sister and me out this time.

Even though he was an alcoholic, he had put his head back on his shoulders long enough to prove to the courts that he could be responsible for us children.

He was still my hero.

My dad.

We only lived with Jack for about six months.

During this time, we lived next door to our Aunt Cindy and our older cousin Luke. Aunt Cindy had given birth to Luke when she was just 12 years old.

While her friends were playing with Barbie dolls, she was trying to raise a child.

So, Aunt Cindy and our cousin Luke were more like brother and sister than mother and son because they were so close in age.

To make things even more complicated (and sick), Luke's father was Mike Colson — my biological father Peter's brother. Mike was in his mid-20s when my then 11-year-old aunt got pregnant.

He denied being the father and threatened Aunt Cindy, trying to pressure her to have an abortion. She still had Luke, so Mike disappeared and never claimed his son.

Luke was never raised as a Colson. And even to his dying day, Mike said he wasn't the father.

But, if you think of it, Luke's blood and my blood are pretty much the same. We are more like brothers than cousins because our fathers were brothers and our mothers were sisters.

This still trips me out.

Although we shared a lot of 'blood,' Luke always picked on me. He would smack me around, put me in headlocks, or just show me his new karate moves by putting his foot into my chest.

One day Aunt Cindy came over to the house and noticed my sister picking up a beer and acting funny. Melissa was tipsy.

She called Child Protective Services (CPS). Our dad was detained, and we were sent back into the foster care system.

It seemed like this went on throughout most of our childhood.

In and out. Back and forth.

Friends were made. Friends were lost.

We were the lost. We were the forgotten.

We were still the unwanted and unloved.

Melissa and I were always going to different schools in different towns.

Sometimes we would be in the same foster home. Other times we would not see one another for months on end.

We were always wondering where our little brother was.

"Where was Eli?"

Where was our curly-haired, strawberry blond little man? Was he still with his evil father? Did he miss us too? Was he safe?

Would we ever see him again?

A SECOND VISION FOR A BETTER FUTURE

Another Glimpse at a Dream Life

To my surprise, my mother's brother and his beautiful wife (Uncle Ron and Aunt Jan) took me out of the system and gave me another chance.

They lived the dream life. They had a beautiful home and were beautiful people with two beautiful children: Shey and Brandan.

Still about 10 years old, and I thought I was living inside a fairytale.

I hoped nobody would pinch me and wake me from this dream.

Just when I thought it could not get any better, Aunt Jan's parents decided that they wanted to adopt me.

The house they lived in was huge. They gave me a room to call my own. I remember it to this very day, furnished with two beds as well as a television and VCR.

Can you imagine that? A television in my own room! Two beds for just me? I felt like I was living in an episode of *Silver Spoons* and I wondered if I were the new Ricky Schroeder (the child star of that TV show).

Their home also had a train that went all the way around their pool. They took me to Knott's Berry Farm (an incredible amusement park in the area). I still pinch myself thinking back. Was this a dream?

They were kind and caring people and wanted to give this kid the dream life he had always envisioned and had always wanted.

I believed I was well on my way.

The Dream Snatched Away

But then their family bickered, fretted about inheritances, and wondered where I would fit into the equation.

Plus, they told me that I would not be able to see or speak to my mother ever again if they were to adopt me. I didn't want that.

As a child, you always hold out hope that your parents can change, grow, evolve, and kick their bad habits. We want the best for those we love.

But my hopes were nothing more than wishful thinking, the dreaming of a young child who always wanted to see the good in others.

No adoption took place, and I was let loose again. It was a short-lived dream life, and I was back into the system.

I still felt like a nameless child. I was still the bastard — not entirely a Colson, not allowed to be a Van Horn, and now, not worthy of taking the name of this family either.

Who was I? What was I?

Where did I fit in this world?

I was again unwanted and unloved like I always was.

How could I find my way in this tumultuous world?

Why was this beautiful life presented to me just to be pulled back?

Was this some sort of cruel joke?

Let's torment this poor, lost little boy once again.

Silver Lining

But the positive thing that this experience did was give me a taste of the life I would eventually pursue and try to emulate. It gave me a view of the life I envisioned that would someday be mine.

I would fight, scratch, and give my heart and soul. This all could be mine.

I did not only want this life I had a glimpse of, but I also wanted even more.

I wanted so much more.

I wanted the home. I wanted the family. I wanted to grab this world and own it. I wanted to make this life mine, determined by me alone.

The bad times in my childhood would not define me.

Instead, they were my driving force and grew my determination to surpass all expectations. It put the fire under my young ass that still burns to this day.

Jimmy Colson

I was all of 10 years old.

Life had thrown me so many curve balls that my head spun around in circles. Life was nothing more than a blur.

I felt like I was on a roller coaster.

One minute we were welfare checks for a foster parent, the next I was told I was from Mars, and the next I was thrust back into the cold, hard reality of a terrible situation.

When would this roller coaster stop?

Could I ever swim out of these dark depths?

SEEDS OF ENTREPRENEURISM

Needing to Make My Own Money

Still about 10 years old, my friends and I started going out to a little creek in San Dimas, California and catch crawdad or clams.

Then, we would pull them in our little red rider wagon out in front of a 7-Eleven convenience store and sell them to people who were going fishing.

It was my first attempt at figuring out how to make my own money. It felt exhilarating. I felt in control.

It was my first entrepreneurial endeavor, but definitely not my last.

Could this be a part of my path out?

The seeds of entrepreneurism had been planted.

SISTER PAYS THE PRICE FOR TAKING US IN

Sister Takes Us In

After being bounced around a lot, the cousin of my Gma on my mom's side extended her hand and took my mom, my sister, and me in. She was the elderly lady we called Sister (who was technically our great-aunt, but we also referred to her as our aunt). She's the same person who, with her mother, took in my mom and her two siblings not kept by my Gma when they were children.

"Sister" was her nickname because she was very religious and sacrificed her whole life to better the lives of all the children she rescued, loved, spoiled, and nurtured.

Sister lived into her 70s and died a virgin. She gave so much that she never learned to live fully, at least not for herself. She never knew a man's touch. She never traveled and never really got to enjoy life outside of her selfless sacrifice for others.

I love and miss her to this very day. She was a like a second mother to me.

Sister was who I learned to love all sports with. Jack taught me to love football, but Sister taught me about all other sports.

We would watch Magic Johnson throw passes to Kareem Abdul-Jabbar or James Worthy on a fast break. We would watch the Dodgers and see Ron Cey or Steve Garvey crank a home run. We would watch Fernando look up to the sky when he threw his screwball. I loved talking with her about it all.

Sister also watched Soap Operas. We watched them almost religiously. Those were wonderful times that I got to spend with her.

She loved Melissa, Eli, and me with all of her heart.

Sister always wanted to make the world better for other people, even if it cost her her own happiness. She always put others before herself.

We lived with her for about a year in a little trailer park in West Covina, California.

Eli Gone for Good

Right around Christmas time, we were so happy to get to see our brother Eli finally after missing him for a long time. His father Jim brought him over to the trailer for a few days, and we got to open some presents together.

But this would be the last place I ever saw my brother Eli until he turned 18. I still remember that day. The last time I saw him, he had tears rolling down his eyes. Just five years old and Jim was smacking him around in front of us.

I wish I could have protected him. Jim was cruel. He was abusive physically and mentally. He was a predator.

Sister tried to stop the abuse too. She weighed about 300 pounds and was close to 70 years old, but Jim slapped her around too. He took off with Eli before the police could arrive.

That was it. I still cannot believe that my little brother was taken away from all of us. I never got to teach Eli to ride a bike. I never got to show him how to swim or how to hit a baseball — so many things I had envisioned doing together just disappeared right before my very eyes.

I lost my brother and a piece of me at the same time.

How We Got Food to Survive

We kids were only able to eat thanks to the Mormon church. Because Sister was Mormon, they gave our family food. Deseret canned food, to be exact. We got peaches, pears, and veggies. It kept us alive while our mom sold her food stamps for her next fix.

Addicts like my mom always sold their food stamps two-for-one back then. For every two food stamps given, my mom would get a dollar in cash back. Then, she'd use the money for drugs.

I am forever grateful for what the church did for us, giving us children food. Without them, we may have starved.

But still, Melissa and I were always very hungry and had to dig through trash cans for extra food. We would go through the trash behind grocery stores finding old candies, broken toys, and so many other cool things that we could not figure out why the stores would throw away.

To us, these were treasures. Junk for some people, they were like pure gold to us.

During the summer of 1984, the United States hosted the Olympics and McDonald's had a promotion where you pulled the tabs off of the drinks or hamburgers to win food whenever the U.S. earned a gold, silver, or bronze medal.

Russia was not at these Olympic games, so we ate McDonald's every day! Sometimes McDonald's fast food was the only thing my sister, Sister, and I would eat all day.

Any extra winning food tickets we had we would use to trade with our friends for small toys.

We were already learning to hustle at a very young age.

Mom's Evil Crew

My mother and her friends (a band of drug addicts I will tell you more about soon) tormented Sister. They stole from her too. It started with a few trinkets going missing. It progressively got worse. They ended up stealing everything she owned.

This poor lady gave all that she could of herself, and now she was robbed blind. Robbed by someone she bestowed so much kindness and love onto.

I also remember my mother kicking, slapping, and spitting in Sister's face. This happened a lot. She called her fat, old, and ugly. She teased her about never feeling a man's touch.

My beautiful mother had turned into a rabid beast. Her words cut through people like a sharp knife.

Even we kids were nothing more than "whiny little shits" to her then. Now known as Skeletor, she had lost her shape and her soul; she was nothing more than skin and a bag of bitter, drugged up bones.

This whole situation was despicable. Sister had raised this woman and two of her siblings as if they were her own. She fed them, bathed them, and tucked them in at night, more of a mother to her than Gma ever was.

But my mom was cruel and only thought of where she could get her next fix.

A Terrible Birthday

I will never forget my 12th birthday party. It was my mother's birthday also if you remember.

Sharing a birthday with your mother can be a blessing or a curse.

This birthday was filled with shady characters waiting for my mom to leave with them so they could all start their hustle for the day (begging for money to use for drugs). My mother had sent out an invite to all of my friends to come over to our trailer. It wasn't to celebrate with me though.

I sat there with no presents from my mother, watching her slide out the side door to "get me a birthday cake." But she didn't come home until the next day.

My friends had come over too. We had no cake, and I had no presents. All I got from my mother for my birthday was misery and embarrassment. I was humiliated and felt so alone. After that, I was teased in school mercilessly.

This is when suicide first entered my mind. I was a shy kid and did not have many friends. I was stuck in a world I believed I was better than, yet could not find an escape from.

My mother would tell us she loved us one minute and the very next minute she would say, "You are going to make me kill myself!" I hope you see the pattern here too. My mother always threatened suicide, so it became a viable option for me as well.

We as parents can project our fears, our insecurities, and our bad habits onto our children.

But, on the positive end, we can also project our pride, our manners, and, most of all our love on them too.

Please be careful in which direction you choose to go. My mother chose both directions. Early on, it leaned toward the positives, later it swayed mostly negative. My mother had become greedy, selfish, and mean.

But she was still our Mommy.

Getting a Fix Above All Else

At Christmas time, we always got presents donated from charities. But when we went back to school, the presents would disappear. My mother saved the boxes to our gifts so that they could be returned for cash. No toy was ever safe in our house. Nothing was safe.

Our mother would also write sympathetic, manipulative letters to the television stations, radio stations, and churches. All to get money for drugs.

Whenever she got money from charities, she used her newfound cash for yet another fix.

Drug addicts have an insatiable appetite for their drugs. They often have no conscience or remorse. They do not see the path of destruction they leave in their wake until it is usually much too late.

They do not see the whole picture. They live in a tunnel vision universe connecting point A (their desire for the drugs) to point B (their acquisition and use of said drugs).

Nothing else matters.

Sister Loses Everything

Now Sister was brought into all of this torture too.

She paid the price for opening her home. Sister was threatened with starvation if she did not do what my mother and her evil crew demanded.

All she had after my mother's wrath was her little dog Poncho and a few picture albums. Sister lost everything else: her trailer, her belongings, her sanity.

Her entire life's possessions were pawned and traded for drugs. Over 60 years of her life were all put into a spoon, lit with a lighter, and mainlined into the arms of my mother and her friends.

Sister's antiques? Traded for a fix.

Her knick-knacks? Sold off for pills.

They could barter anything for drugs.

At this time, my mother got onto another welfare program managed by the U.S. Department of Housing and Urban Development (HUD) called Section 8. Essentially, her rent was subsidized by the government and was only $80 per month. But the landlord would work with her and the tenants to rip off the government with false rent values. For example, they would raise the rental prices, but not take additional money from the tenants, just to get more money from the government.

So, our family now had a 3-bedroom house. It was in a purely Hispanic neighborhood in Palmdale, California. This was the new hub for all the addicts. We were in what some would consider the ghetto. I would end up making it my home.

Sister moved in with us because her trailer was sold out from under her.

My mom got further and further into drugs. Now she was slamming cocaine with heroin, doing dangerous concoctions they called speedballs. The heroin worked as a downer, the cocaine as an upper. Users did not know whether they were coming or going. Happy or sad. My mother and her crew had their new addiction, and it was a dangerous one.

It takes so many lives. It destroys so many childhoods. It turns good people bad.

It got to the point where they would force me to tie their arms off with a belt while they slammed one another. Blood would squirt on me, my sister, and my aunt.

My clothes had small blood stains, and the unfathomable memories will last much longer than any of those stains ever could. The imprints they left on my mind are undeniable.

The imprints they left on my soul are eternal.

BOYFRIEND 2: LIMP DICK PRICK - JAMES

Mom's Next Boyfriend

A part of the evil crew, mom's new boyfriend was a terrible man named James.

She called him "Limp Dick Prick."

He was an ex-military man and a firefighter. He had two children of his own, Anthony and Kendi. And he was also a heroin addict like my mom.

Together, my mother and James ran the evil crew, which consisted of the man I told you about earlier in his tighty-whities named Gary, a mellow guy named Danny, and a couple of hyped up speed freaks whose names left my mind many years ago.

They were all thieves. But they worked together to leverage their efforts.

Each day they would plot out the course of events for us. Sister, Melissa, and I were forced to head out with criminal assignments, each of us in one of three groups.

1. One group was the thieves.

The evil crew would scout out stores, pick things to take, grab price tags off of the same item, steal it, bring it back to the car, and then force us to return it for the money.

Imagine that. Sister (70 years old), Melissa (10 years old), and I (12 years old) were forced to sit in the car while they stole as much as they could, only to send us back in to return it all that same day for cash.

They stole cologne, Preparation H, and other small things for which they could easily get money back.

They even purchased some products and made copies of the receipts. Then, they would wet them to make it look as if they went through a washing machine, giving us a chance to get a refund when we took the worn-looking receipts back in with the stolen items of the same product.

2. The next group was the panhandlers.

They forced my little sister and me to beg for money with them on street corners, in between our taking back stolen merchandise from group 1.

They would beg from people we knew, like neighbors and even other children. They had no remorse, compassion, or conscience.

3. The third group would go from church to church.

They dragged us with them from church to church, saying that we were hungry, our electricity was about to be shut off, the water bill was due, the car was broken down, or we just needed a tank of gas. Sometimes we had to go in alone and claim to need money because we were starving or cold.

You get the point.

Sometimes what we said was true, other times not entirely.

The churches would help by giving us food or money, paying our bills, filling the tank with gas, or helping any way they possibly could. And it did not matter what denomination the church was. The crew did not care. Everyone had money ripe for the taking.

And even though we were given charity money to buy food, that is not what we got. My mother and her evil crew did not care if we had nothing to eat. They were quintessential hustlers. They had to be, with such an insatiable appetite for so many drugs.

Only One Priority

This crew worked like a well-oiled machine.

They cleared between $500 to $1000 a day. Tax-free. They took no days off. No amount of money would ever be enough to satiate their hunger for drugs. Their machine transformed good deeds into blazing syringes with no conscience.

Until that needle pricked a hole, the world was on hold.

Until the drugs entered their veins, we were like everyone else: a pawn in their evil game they called life.

The crew had no one to answer to either, besides the demons in their arms and the weakness of their minds, hearts, and souls. Our voices were never heard. Our cries were never answered. We were the voiceless and we were the damned.

Still, my sister, our aunt, and I were along for this ride. They would curse at Sister for gaining weight and now needing a walker everywhere we went out to hustle because it took up space in the Pinto. Five of us were already stuffed in the little car, and now we had to squeeze a walker in with us too.

We were all just another way for them to get their next fix.

This crew had no concern about our missing school. They did not care if we were held back, if we failed classes, or if we were taken away from our mother.

They did not care how far down the depths they sank. How far they pulled us down.

Teachers just shook their heads and did the best they could with us for how many absences we always had. There was no way we could keep up.

Our mother's demons always needed to be fed. All else in life was secondary. We were secondary. We were the unwanted and unloved.

The Car Wash Incident

One day, Mr. Tighty-Whitey (Gary from earlier), our mother, a friend of mine named Hector, and I were in the Valley panhandling and taking back stolen merchandise when we pulled into a car wash.

We kids were forced to tie my mother's and her friends' arms off so that they could get their fix again.

Black tar in a spoon and a cigarette butt ripped open (as their skin soon would be).

We watched them heat the spoon from the bottom with a lighter.

We watched the sweat drip from their brows and the color of their eyes fade into the darkness. The darkness they were adding into their bloodstreams. The darkness we kids would once again endure.

The man in the car behind us kept honking his horn because we were blocking the entrance.

Mr. Tighty-Whitey got out of the car, ripped his plaid shirt completely in half, and ran at the man, with the belt still tied around his arm.

It was unbelievable. It was inconceivable.

Gary chased the car out of the parking lot. I saw the fear on that man's face. His fears were well warranted.

Gary had increased strength from the numbing of the drugs and had no regard for authority. No fear. No concern about the consequences of his actions.

Gary wanted his fix and was going to get it at any cost even if he had to knock down mountains and destroy lives. That needle needed to tear a hole, and it needed to be done at that moment.

No one would stop him from the fleeting euphoria that he and the whole crew chased.

The man in the car behind us had seen Gary's demons firsthand and did not want to stick around and face the consequences.

My friend Hector and I had to hitchhike to get a ride back home from the Valley all the way to Palmdale (about 50 miles). Luckily, a nice newlywed couple picked us up from the side of the road.

This crazy episode was only one instance of many that I was dragged into. Melissa and I were lucky we lived through it all.

This Time It's Different

But this time I had had enough.

I decided to stand up to my mother and her crew.

If we had to take back stolen merchandise, then we deserved 33% of the money, or they could go into the stores wearing their filthy bell bottom pants and tube tops. They knew that the managers would refuse to issue them refunds because the stores saw them as the thieves that they were.

The crew was angry and felt betrayed. We were happy and felt vindicated because Sister, Melissa, and I could use our cut to buy food and clothes.

Now, we did not have to steal food to survive. We did not need to eat bread with mustard on it, pretending it was a real sandwich. We did not need to find ways of making the Deseret canned vegetables seem like a full meal.

Overdosing

During this tough time, our mother was, unsurprisingly, always teetering on death from all of the drugs. We often had to carry her to the shower with a syringe still hanging out from her arm.

She overdosed more than a few times.

Melissa and I would try to make sure she didn't choke on her tongue as her eyes rolled back into her head. We never knew if our mom would make it through each day, let alone live through our whole childhoods.

My mother's crew of addicts went into panic-mode every time someone overdosed. Although they never lost anyone from their crew while they were working together, through the years, one fell right after another.

Drugs always get their victim, if the user never wakes from their evil hold. Drugs seemingly give you an escape from life. But in the eyes of your child, drugs rip out your heart and your soul.

Death then, ironically, is a life act for those in the crosshairs of a heroin addict.

My mom would go with her so-called friends to methadone clinics to get another fix. Another fix added on top of the ones that they were already getting.

Their comedowns were insane and lasted until the next needle tore its hole.

You would not believe how many drugs they did. But it was never enough.

My mother would cry and beg me for all of my money. She would be covered in sweat and trying to get whatever little bit of drugs she could out of the used cotton balls and syringes lying around.

She would soil herself, pee herself, vomit, cry, and scream hysterically.

We experienced so many days and nights of nonstop begging and crying.

She would call me every name in the book and say she wished she had never even given birth to us. Once that needle tore its hole we were welcome again. We were loved and wanted now.

Innocence Lost

Our mother's hunger for her next fix had grown insatiable. It was uncontrollable. She had no concern for the path of destruction it was carving out for Melissa and me.

We could only imagine what our little brother was going through too. I prayed for him every single night.

As I think back, what is considered a child? A child is someone whose parents nurture and protect. A child is someone who looks at life through rose-colored glasses. If that is the definition, then we had not been children for a very long time.

We were more of hustlers ourselves. We had to be.

I would always have to give my money to my mom so that she and James would not pawn the television again. So that they would not sell all of our food stamps and let us go hungry.

Most of our "childhood" was like this.

A long line of watching my mom and her many men get so high that they never seemed like they would ever come down. My mother even had the drug dealers pick up Melissa, now only 10 years old, and drive her around for the day as they sold drugs.

Melissa would sit in the passenger seat, and they'd drive off.

I have never asked her what happened once they left. I don't even know if I could handle the answer. She has enough scars. Why open up Pandora's box and expose it to the world?

My poor little sister was thrown in as the entertainment.

In exchange? The dealers passed my mom a small balloon wrapped tightly with a ball of black tar heroin inside.

My baby sister and her innocence were traded for nothing more than another fix.

Our mother sold her soul. She sold her children. She sold her life for the needle, for the escape.

She would sell anything for another fix.

Finally, I had enough and started to drift into an entirely different world. I was sick of walking down the street and getting called names, beat up, and harassed. I needed some kind of escape, and it needed to start now.

That is when I started hanging out with friends in a Hispanic gang. They looked out for me. Maybe I was one of them; perhaps I was more of a pet or a mascot.

All I knew was I was now safe, I was fed, and I was happy.

PART 4
TEENAGE TRIBULATIONS

13 YEARS OLD: WITH A GANG

One Darkness for Another Darkness

I was now 13 and felt on top of the world. I was even getting good grades in school despite all of the excessive absences and hanging with gang kids. I was happy. But that was about to change.

I had been to the other side. I was in numerous fights, I was protected, I started to smoke marijuana, and I drank daily. I felt as if I was one of them, part of a family. They called me "Mr. Chiclets" because I stuck to my friends like gum.

This was going on for over a year.

I remember buying the first Ruthless Record out of the trunk of Eazy-E's Impala with my friends Lil Smiley and Toy. One day while at the park, I tried to get someone in a headlock and got stabbed. It was a big rumble with ten or more guys involved. I still have the scar to this day. It was not a deep wound, but it definitely was a wakeup call.

My life was now not my own. I was running with something much bigger, a gang, a family, and I needed to earn their respect. I had been hit with baseball bats, struck with sticks, stabbed, and even shot at.

This was now a part of life.

I went from not knowing where my next meal was going to come from, to life or death in a whole other way. One darkness for another darkness.

FROM THE DEPTHS

We had carloads of friends driving around starting fights. We had no remorse either. At least they did not. I always felt horrible. I hated hurting others, but I always struck back when challenged.

These times were tough, but at least when I was out with my friends, I did not have to deal with my mother, her screaming, her cursing, all of her crying, and the insults that cut deep into your soul like a sharpened knife.

That was a daily ritual until it was time to lay my head down at night.

The police would often show up, and if we mouthed off, we would take a flashlight to our knees. I was told, "That won't leave a mark. So, shut up you little ghetto piece of shit."

I remember my sister coming home with hickeys on her neck. She was rolling around in the bushes with two other little boys. She was only 12 years old then.

So, I confronted her, and while lecturing her, she picked up our ironing board and struck me across my kneecaps. I fell to the ground, and she punched me square in the face.

As I lay there in pain, she laughed and ran out the door and down the street. Later that evening I saw her and popped her one right back.

Right at that moment my mom walked in and grabbed a broomstick. She smacked me with it and chased me around the house, hitting me repeatedly.

She then told me I disgusted her and threw me out.

14 YEARS OLD: ON THE STREET AND SUICIDAL

Homeless

I was now 14 and essentially living on the streets for the first, but not the last, time. I slept in an abandoned house down our street and would go to my friend Angel's house to eat and bathe.

It was just a little taste of freedom, even though it came at a price.

On the Edge

I left a suicide note on my old bed, and my mother let me back in the house. Times were tough, and so was each life lesson. Most children who kill themselves do it out of feeling unloved. They feel lost and alone.

You Are Not Alone

One of the main reasons I wrote this book is the hope to save at least one life by sharing my story. To know that all of these trials could aid just one kid by sharing them? To help one kid to see hope and grow?

Never feel alone and remember that tomorrow always offers something you might not feel today.

That is the gift of hope.

Hope can move mountains.

Hope can change outcomes and give you strength.

Thus, never give up hope. Even if I almost did.

I always did what I wanted, when I wanted. I wore a gold chain with a cross. I was also the first kid on my street to own a Nintendo. I ate whatever I wanted. I had found my own hustles and was making money any way I could, including selling marijuana.

Out on the streets, at least I did not have to deal with the drug addicts in my house. I did what I had to do to survive.

MELISSA GETS CAUGHT SELLING DRUGS

Our "Hustles"

Melissa and I had both found multiple sources of income. Learning how to hustle and make money meant we did not have to worry where our next meal was going to come from anymore.

Unfortunately, she started selling drugs much worse than marijuana.

But we were both finding our way in this cruel, unforgiving world. Melissa and I were and always will be survivors. We know how to work for what we want and need.

For example, I would walk down the street with a shopping cart selling candy and soda (and I had marijuana on me too). At school, I would sell candy, baseball cards, and football cards.

With all my side hustles, I was taking in between $100 to $200 every day.

Not bad for a poor 14-year-old kid. I had found a calling.

I had learned not to be so shy from having to take back stolen merchandise for all of those years. So selling collectible cards? It was easy.

I could sell anyone a card with a little charm. I'd buy common cards of players from the 1960s or 1970s and talk them way up.

My friends stole money from their parents just to get baseball cards or candies from me. I felt as if I could do or buy anything I ever wanted.

That is, of course, until my mother needed her next fix and took all of my money from me.

She would scream, cry, and beg. Anything for her next fix. Anything to help her escape herself, even if it were only for a minute. She believed that she had bugs in her arms and ripped her flesh away.

She was deteriorating right in front of us.

Melissa Gets Busted

But it was my sister who was the first of us to get popped by an undercover sting. At 12 years old, Melissa was locked up for selling crack cocaine to an undercover police officer.

She went right back into the system.

But this time it was not a foster home, this was Juvenile Hall. Melissa was young and tough. Her street smarts and will to live have always been second-to-none. She is a product of our environment. She will always be a survivor.

I was next in line to be taken away. It was a never-ending cycle. We were out of school just as much as we were in school. I have no idea how I kept good grades during such trying times.

On the positive side, this chaos forced me to learn how to multitask, a skill that has helped me throughout my life ever since.

As much school as I missed, I still knew academics were very important. Knowledge is the one thing that will keep you ahead in life. Knowledge comes in all forms, shapes, and sizes.

You have street smarts, book smarts, and the least common of them all: common sense.

Learning will be your blessing and it will give you that extra push into greatness.

Never give up on your thirst for knowledge. Feed that hunger, and you can live your life without limits. If others give up on you, that is their mistake. Not yours.

Never give up on yourself. You know your own worth.

Never give up on your dreams.

Use learning and knowledge to help you get to where you want to go.

MORTIFYING SCHOOL ASSEMBLY

Utter Shame

I tried to do as best as I could in school when I was there. But living on the streets half the time and with drugged out "parents" the other half didn't make it easy.

The only thing that could make my school experience worse would be if my school life and home life collided.

It did.

One school assembly still haunts me. It was an awards assembly where the children were on one side of the auditorium, and the parents were on the opposite side.

All of the sudden the doors swung open and the sunlight filled the room. Who could be so rude as to show up mid-assembly?

It was my mother and her boyfriend James in their filthy bell bottom pants. My mom also had on a yellow tube top that was grungy and dirty.

I can still picture them as they walked into the auditorium. They had stopped their hustling long enough to come in to congratulate me.

But I tried not to let anyone know that, yes, the panhandlers were with me.

Yes, the people who beg for your money are mine. Or, at least, I was theirs.

These two junkies were there to make sure that even at school I had no escape. I had nowhere to run. I had nowhere to hide. I was mortified.

"Jimmy? Jimmy, where are you? We want to tell you congratulations and we love you!"

I sank deeper and deeper into my chair. At that moment, whatever little pride I had all but vanished. I was so embarrassed and ashamed of who I was and where I came from.

Was there any hope for a poor kid like me? Did any of us three children stand a chance in this life? My mother and James brought it to my school for all to see.

Kids were cracking up and pointing.

Parents were whispering and shaking their heads.

The principal had to stop the assembly to ask my mother and James to sit down in the parent section.

I wanted to die at that very moment.

The Beginning of the End

The damage was done, and I wanted as far away from school as I could get. I was so humiliated and could not even face the few friends that I did have.

Later, parents would not let their children be anywhere around me because of where I came from.

I was the panhandlers' kid.

FROM THE DEPTHS

The parents had every right to want to shield their children from what I was a part of — they did not want the innocence of their little ones to be lost too.

I wish that we all lived in a world where you are not judged by your origins, which you cannot control. Instead, we should all be judged on where we want to ascend to and who we want to become. I knew I would shoot for the stars and arrive.

Someday I would be given a chance.

That day was definitely not today.

This was the beginning of the end for me in school.

HIT BY PIZZA DRIVER + CPS

45 Minutes or Less

To make matters worse, I was also hit by a pizza delivery driver who had to deliver his pizza in 45 minutes or less. He backed out of the parking lot without looking and backed over me.

My friend Hector punched the driver's car to stop him and prevent him from completely running me down. The driver replied, "Take it up with my manager. I have a pizza to deliver, kid."

Can you believe that?

When the police arrived, they classified it as a hit and run. The driver got into a lot of trouble.

$500

The big pizza company, not wanting any bad publicity, called a meeting with my mother and James.

They showed up grungy and looking for money for their next fix. They both wore dirty bell bottom jeans, and my mother had on her everyday tube top. They looked as if they had not bathed in a week. You could see the desperation and smell the filth. They would not leave without money in hand.

So the pizza company, I am sure, chuckled when my mother and James accepted a mere $500 settlement. They gave up all of my legal rights for a measly $500.

I spoke with lawyer friends of mine later on in life, and they told me that I had a great lawsuit and if my mother had not been so desperate I would have been set up for a long time. Just 45 minutes or less could have set me up financially for 45 years or more.

Child Protective Services

Not too long after the $500 settlement, I got a bad rash near my testicles that was in the shape of a circle. I was scared to death, but my mother refused to take me to the hospital because it would affect my being able to be the money maker in her hustles.

I was worried, I was scared, and I was lost. I did not know what I was going to do.

A few days later, the doorbell rang. It was Child Protective Services to take my sister and me back into custody. My mother and Melissa ran out the back door and into the desert. I stayed and decided to let them take me away.

They said I was incorrigible and had no business running the streets. Looking back, that was a great description of me. They knew what I was doing, yet they had no proof. I really needed to get my rash looked at and could think of no other way.

My 70-year-old aunt Sister was screaming and crying. It was a total madhouse — people escaping, others left behind.

My poor aunt had no one to protect her when I left.

Jimmy Colson

THE BOYS HOME + RUNNING AWAY

A Bad New Start

The rash turned out to be nothing more than ringworm and was easily cured. I wanted a new start and hoped this would be it. I was looking for a little hope.

That is when they decided it was best to put me in a boys home: the Community Group Home for Boys in Palmdale, California. I was about to start my freshman year of high school and was now in State custody.

At the time, I was the youngest child there. I was all of a hardened 14 years of age with a chip on my shoulder that would soon be knocked off, repeatedly. This boys home had 10 kids, and we all had different stories. All had affiliations with different gangs from around the greater Los Angeles area. We even had a white supremacist thrown in for the fun of it, I guess.

What a rag-tag motley crew of misfits we were.

But this was to be my new home.

Our house parents were Pops and Betty. Pops was an older, heavyset man with a Southern drawl in his late 60s and his wife Betty was a little under 5 feet tall with short hair and a bad attitude.

They ruled the home with an iron fist beyond belief. I am sure this was due to how many children who came and went. They looked you over and stated the rules. What they said was set in stone. No questions asked.

No need to ask a question, they did not answer them anyway. If you did not listen, you would not get your $5 a week for allowance, your home passes, or get to go out on the movie nights. They could also keep your snacks.

It is funny when you look back and realize they could control you with so little to lose. I went from having hundreds of dollars in my pocket to being the best kid I could be for five bucks a week.

The first few weeks were pure hell. I wondered if I had made a huge mistake.

Who lets themselves get taken into custody? Who would voluntarily say, 'Yes, it is me, take me away'? And was I leaving one hell just to enter into another?

I was so used to being in gang-style fights that I did not know how to fight on my own. I got beat up pretty regularly. I fought back to no avail.

These were 17-year-olds with chips on their shoulders and fists with my name on them. These were tough-as-nails kids who all lived similar lives to mine. We were all the lost, the forgotten, and the unwanted.

We were all in too deep.

Tortured

I remember being woken up at night and being choked, fighting to keep my gold chain. I remember walking into the hall and being punched in the gut. And when they would walk by, they would kick me and laugh.

I got boogers flicked at me at night and woke up with them stuck to my forehead and all over my face. They would roll up newspapers and stick them in my nose while I slept too. It was a never-ending nightmare. You'd have to sleep with one eye open at all times.

I remember going to brush my teeth only to see pubic hair in my toothbrush and semen on the soap.

Life is cruel sometimes. Broken children can be even crueler.

This was an awakening for me. I learned to conquer my fears and realized that I had enough. I would not let them take control of me.

But life turned into a game of cat and mouse just to bathe or brush my teeth. Each day, I resolved to walk into the desert surrounding the boys home and bury my soap, toothbrush, and toothpaste. I marked my spots with a rock. Then, I got up early to dig it up and get ready for school.

I would not be defeated by these disgusting pranks. I would not let them. They would not own me. I own my destiny.

I was strong, but there was no way I could take this much longer.

Homecoming Dance

Most of us kids came from bad upbringings and had just as bad of attitudes. But we all wanted freedom. The boys home gave us a chance at a little bit of freedom with home passes for weekends if you did all of your chores and pretty much kissed up to what they had to say or wanted you to do. They said, "Jump!" and you would be screwed if you did not reply, "How high?"

I remember getting my first home pass the same weekend as the Homecoming dance. I asked a girl to go with me. I could not believe that she said yes.

I was so nervous and excited. I was still shy at this point in life, and this was a big accomplishment for me.

I was locked up but still going to go to Homecoming. I told one of my fellow boys home rejects, and he said, "Are you excited? Man, she is so beautiful." And then he punched me in the face and split my lip right in half.

He ruined my weekend. He cost me my home pass for fighting, and I did not get to go to the dance. I was ashamed and embarrassed. I did not stand up to him. I was scared, unwanted, and unloved.

Despite my physical and mental pain, he just laughed hysterically. He was not worried about home passes. He had nothing to lose and nowhere to go. He said, and I still remember it to this day, "Now you won't be so pretty for her, will you?"

Hot Iron Ass Whooping

A few days later, the biggest guy in the boys home picked a fight with me. As I was defending myself, his best friend (who had been ironing his pants) hit me with the scolding hot iron. It was steaming hot and blistered my skin.

I can still remember the pain and the smell of my burning flesh. I stood there in disbelief as the two of them pummeled me to the ground. They beat me to a bloody pulp. I was in so much agony and pain. My arm scarred, my lip busted, and my ass whooped.

I learned though that even an ass whooping would not deter me.

Life was tough during those dark days. I dealt with depression and suicidal thoughts almost daily.

Would It Ever Get Better?

I had to believe life could be better than this. That I could be better than this.

To escape for just a little while, we kids would steal wire cutters and cut open the fence surrounding the boys home. We cut a hole where no one ever went.

It gave us a little opening to sneak through and go goof off in the tunnels under the California Aqueduct.

Go in one side locked up, come out the other a free man.

Even if that freedom lasted only a couple of hours, we were free.

Free of the tyranny of the home.

We were free of the house parents who were deep asleep.

When we sneaked out, we were a team. No ass whoopings. Instead, we all looked out for one another.

We were fenced in on this large piece of property with no neighbors for a couple of blocks. We would sneak out at night and go for long walks, meet up with girls from school, or even break into other people's homes.

Or we'd break into other boys homes when we knew the house parents were on vacation. When they went out of town, they would put the kids in other homes like ours. And kids always know where the treats are.

We'd steal those Little Debbie's snack packs that we all had to be so good for. Heck, we would break in and eat a whole box apiece.

This was a way of getting more than the $5 a week they gave us as an allowance.

Life at 14

Fourteen years old and I could not afford to do my hair, buy any clothes, or get food. We were unable to do anything at all.

They treated us like dogs.

We were nothing more than paychecks to them. It was never a good environment.

I remember girls from my high school who liked me would call things off. I could not do anything except see them at school or, if they were able to sneak out at night, we could get just a few minutes alone.

A girl I was trying to date went for my best friend David, and she had sex with him behind the movie theaters. I could not even be mad at either of them.

I had no life at all.

Depression started to get the best of me. I had to fight to keep my mind right.

This was wake up, go to school, go back to the boys home to do all of my chores — rinse and repeat.

They also sent psychiatrists to speak with us weekly to psychoanalyze us and tell us what we needed to work on. It seemed like they would never actually listen, just tell you what was required of you.

You could tell them you were depressed or suicidal and they seemed to think that *that* was your problem.

You caused these thoughts and needed to find a way out of your own head. You were why you were in the situation you were in.

They would tell you how you needed to handle the situation at hand and grow. How could they tell us anything when we had no voice?

One Summer

The parents at the boys home got a handful of us kids to work a summer job at our high school. I was one of the lucky few chosen.

We had to do all of the gardening: mowing lawns, trimming hedges, pulling weeds, and tidying everything up.

At least they were teaching us a trade.

It was a great escape for all of us teenagers who were chosen. We were a band of misfits on a mission. We wanted nothing more than to be out of the different boys homes we were each stuck in.

We had a blast together and earned money. They gave us $50 a day for working our butts off in 100-plus degree weather.

I saved up close to $1,000 during that summer. And I had big dreams of buying clothes, hairspray, baseball cards, and so much more.

But during the last weekend of that summer, I had one of my sessions with the home's psychiatrist.

He was an Indian gentleman who carried himself well and had to deal with a lot from all of us teenagers. Once a week, like clockwork, he would show up to the boys home along with his Asian wife.

He had counseling sessions with us kids down to a science. He'd always ask me the same exact questions:

"Have you learned anything new?"

"What have you gotten from this experience?"

This time though, I turned to him and his wife and asked, "Are the two of you married?"

He replied, "Yes we are."

I then retorted, "If you have any children, will they be sushi eating camel jockeys?"

I will never forget that line because they cleared out my bank account to buy curtains for the boys home as punishment. All of my hard work was turned into shade providers.

White with floral print. I can still see them in my mind.

One smart-ass, racist remark cost me everything I had worked hard for. Looking back, I did deserve it, and it was a needed life lesson. And, boy, did I ever learn.

Life lessons are almost never easy on you. And usually, we do not recognize them until we are far away from the situation.

I believe that racism has no place in society and it is sad to still think people are judged by the color of their skin and not the pureness of their hearts. I do regret what I said.

In hindsight, I learned so much during those lonely, misguided days.

I learned how to stand up for myself even if I knew a beating was imminent. I also learned my very first trade (with the landscaping).

We kids were all a part of a mixed group with every race represented. If you were raised with prejudice, this boys home would knock it right out of you.

I also learned to be a young man. I learned to carry myself well and taught myself some manners.

Yet, this did not stop me from being furious. I wanted out of this hole. I also wanted my revenge and vindication.

I wanted to escape and show them all that I was gone and would never look back.

My Escape

So when I got my second home pass, I ran away with my girlfriend, her two beautiful sisters, and her mother.

They were living in the Valley, and I hitchhiked all the way there to join this party.

My girlfriend was a winsome witch I had met before I was in the boys home. A witch, for real. She was a Wiccan, although I had no idea what that was at the time.

She taught me so much and put up with all of my naiveties and insecurities. She was attractive, but she was so different — black lipstick and an attitude.

Her family was heading to Las Vegas that weekend, and I jumped in the car with them, planning to never look back.

Jimmy Colson

LAS VEGAS

Weekend in Vegas

Las Vegas was mesmerizing.

It was called the city of lights for good reason. Breaking through the mountains and seeing the state line for the first time, I thought it was amazing.

Just 30 minutes later, I saw the real Las Vegas and was left breathless. I will never forget seeing the lights for the first time.

I was in awe of the casinos and fell in love.

I had no idea that this was where I would someday call my home. This would be where I would finally start a family and make a life for myself.

At the time, it was more of a dream that I never wanted to wake from. It was an escape from the hell I had been thrown into.

Heck, with three beautiful teenage girls too? I was in heaven, and Las Vegas was my paradise. We partied, drank until we passed out, and made a lot of new friends.

But sadly, this was just a weekend, and when we went back to California, Sister had called and said they were threatening to arrest her.

She spent her life helping everyone, and I could not let her be incarcerated for me.

I Went Back

So, I decided to turn myself in and face the consequences. I could not let this kind lady — who loved me and sacrificed for so many of us — serve time for my being AWOL.

I hitchhiked my way back to the High Desert and turned myself into Pops and Betty. I would endure any and all consequences.

But did I ever have a great journey while it lasted!

I had a taste of freedom that forever changed me.

They took me back in, but I was unable to go on home passes ever again. I was only allowed to leave to go to school. This was going to last until I turned 18 or my mother lost her thirst for heroin. I surely was not holding my breath on that one.

BECOMING ONE OF THE BAD GUYS I DESPISED

The Worst Beating of My Life

The white supremacist roommate I had in the boys home continued to pick on me daily.

He was cruel and singled me out to take his wrath.

He was evil and had a mean streak that I still think of to this very day.

He was the reason that I would wake up with boogers all over my face in the mornings.

I had enough of his torture, so one day I got behind him and put him in a chokehold.

I wanted to kill him.

I wanted to make sure he never picked on anyone ever again.

He had me thinking about suicide all of the time. But I wanted to live. I just did not want to live this life. I did not want to be treated as if I were subhuman.

I was a young man, and I had a voice. Even if it were too faint yet to be heard.

So as I got him in a tight headlock, I figured I would never let go. I would make him pay for all that he did to me.

But then he pulled his chin under my hold and bit me on my arm on the opposite side of my elbow. He bit me right where my arm bent, and he hit a bunch of nerves. I lost feeling in my fingertips, and my hand went spastic. I had no control, and the pain shot up and was unbearable, so I let go.

It was so painful, yet I tried to fight him back with one hand.

He ended up giving me one of the worst beatings of my life. I was black and blue, my ribs were in pain, and my arm and hand would never be the same.

I still have the nerve damage from this savage beating. I cannot write anymore. Not more than a sentence before I feel the pain shooting up my arm. It serves as a daily reminder of that time in life.

He was truly the definition of evil in my book.

Most of the people in the boys home were of different ethnicities, but no one wanted to mess with this guy. He was bad news and was in control.

Unfortunately, he was my roommate and my tormentor.

But he did teach me how to fight. He beat me up and at the same time would show me how to fight. He was cruel but also taught me.

Sometimes the people you hate the most still teach you life lessons.

You can grow from what your enemies put you through. Sometimes that is where you learn and grow the most. They have no filters, no remorse, and no obligation to you or your feelings.

Every moment in life is a learning experience if you allow it to be.

15 Years Old

I had now been in this boys home for over a year.

We all watched our Los Angeles Dodgers win the World Series in 1988. I will never forget seeing Kirk Gibson come to bat hobbled. None of us thought he was going to play.

Once in the game, he did the impossible.

He was given no chance yet homered off of Dennis Eckersley to help the Dodgers win the World Series.

This was the highlight of the year and all my time in the boys home. We were all jumping up and down. White, Black, Hispanic, it did not matter.

We were all winners; we were on our way to a championship.

The unloved had something to hold onto.

Our team was named champion — so that somehow made us champions too. We had that glimmer of hope returned to us. We could escape this hell even if it were only for a moment.

We were free in our minds.

Sports helped me so much throughout my childhood.

I could get lost in the numbers on the back of my baseball cards. I loved to alphabetize the teams and the different card makers. I always had them organized.

My friends and I would go out and steal boxes of cards and sell the ones we did not want.

Becoming What I Despised

Soon after the World Series, I was at school with friends, and a rather large guy tried starting a fight with my friend David. He was upset that someone had thrown a juice at him and his girlfriend.

It was not David or our other friend Mike, but the guy believed it was.

David and Mike were much smaller than he was. And I was smaller still, but I had so much anger built up that I would take on him or anyone who wanted to jump in.

This was the beginning of my becoming the aggressor.

I told the guy to leave my friends alone and if he had a problem, his problem was with me.

He agreed, and it was on.

I was wearing flip-flops and asked a buddy to wear his shoes. I was a size 10.5 at the time (size 13 now), and he had size 13 shoes. We called him the Albino Giant. He was excited and jumped out of his shoes, and I threw them on to fight.

He swung at me as I swung at him. He missed, and I broke his nose. He threw me on the lockers and missed again as I continued to punch him in his ribs. I held him up with one arm while I went to a knee and continued to punch him in his testicles.

My classmates started chanting "Rocky! Rocky!"

I did not realize that I had knocked him out and was holding him up with my arm.

I had just let all my pain and aggression out on this poor guy. He did not deserve such a savage beating.

I had now become one of the bad guys.

I had become what I had despised most. I was the one inflicting pain.

I saw blood on my new shirt and went over and kicked him a few times. I was an animal. I was sick of being beaten.

I was now the aggressor. I was the one to give the beatdowns. I would no longer be beaten. I would give the beatings.

The boys home helped create a monster.

CYA + ESCAPING TO LAS VEGAS

California Youth Affiliate

I went back to the boys home that evening when they received the call. They took me aside and said that the kid was put in the hospital and I was going to be taken by CYA in the morning.

CYA is short for California Youth Affiliate, where the worst of the worst of Los Angeles and surrounding cities' gang members went.

We also called it "Cover Your Ass."

They said that I would be there until I was 18 and proceeded to laugh. They could not believe that I had put such a whooping on a bigger kid. I felt bad but knew I could not make it in CYA. I would be destroyed, beaten, and bloodied. Quickly.

I was not strong enough to live through CYA.

What was my next step? Should I beg? Should I plead?

RUN!

The next morning, about an hour before CYA arrived, the new kid who was taking my place came up to me. He had just gotten kicked out of a different boys home for molesting their poodles.

He was the new kid for them to bully on. He was the new kid to teach how to fight. And now he was yelling at me, "Run!"

I asked him if he was crazy. By now, the CYA van was almost to the boys home.

He said, "If you don't, you will be toast in CYA." He said I was a dead man walking and they would beat me to death in there.

So, I turned my little stereo on and asked for privacy as I packed. I put my flip-flops on, packed my baseball cards and a couple of outfits, and ran.

I ran as if my life depended on it. And to this day, I believe my life did hang in the balance with that decision.

Running hard, I went underneath the California Aqueduct where we had cut the fence with wire cutters. When I came up the other side, I felt as if I were a free man.

I ran until I was out of breath. I then ran some more.

I ended up running all the way to our high school. I ran past the tumbleweeds, past the Joshua trees, and through the rocks.

My feet were bleeding, but I did not care. A little blood lost for freedom was well worth it to me.

This was to be my grand escape.

This would be my chance at a new life, at a new beginning. I had no idea what life had in store. I just knew I wanted more. I wanted to be more. And I believed I deserved more.

By the time I arrived at school, the police, CYA, and all the bouncers at the school were already searching for me. Everyone drove circles around the high school, looking.

FROM THE DEPTHS

I was wanted for the first time in my life. By everyone!

But I was wanted for all of the wrong reasons. I was on the run and had nowhere to go. I had nowhere to hide. I called my best friend David, but he had ditched school that day to go to the mall.

I tossed my baseball cards and other belongings to a friend I saw and continued to run. But I decided to hang out at the school for a little while. Boy, was that ever a big mistake. In between classes I heard a golf cart coming towards me.

It was George. He was ex-military and had a huge afro. We all called him Buckwheat. He said, "I see you, Jimmy, you got nowhere to go."

I kicked off my flip-flops and ran. I ran as fast as I could. My feet bled more and throbbed in pain. I blocked it out and continued to run.

Past the classrooms. Down the halls. But when I made a beeline towards the Future Farmers of America area, I was boxed in.

I was trapped.

At that moment, a new bouncer with broad shoulders who I'd never seen before ran behind me. I froze and stood still. I was the captured. I was the wanted, and I was done.

As he grabbed me and tackled me to the ground, all I could think was if this was it.

Was this the gateway to California Youth Affiliate?

Would this lead to my being incarcerated until I was 18 years old?

So many things ran through my mind on the ride to the principal's office. All that running and now I was headed to CYA. My childhood never existed, but now it was going to get a whole lot worse.

I thought the days and nights in the boys home were bad. That was like Disneyland compared to where they were sending me. They put you in handcuffs daily with prison type food, in a prison-like setting.

George taunted me, called me names, and drove me back to the principal's office where the boys home was waiting.

I said, "Screw you, Buckwheat!" and was on the run again.

Again, I ran through the Future Farmers of America area and was almost tackled a second time.

I ran through the desert barefoot.

My feet were bleeding even worse, and I was exhausted both physically and mentally.

The Escape?

That's when another friend offered to ditch the rest of the day and take me to his house until David came back to town.

We jumped in his car and went to fill his tank with gas.

FROM THE DEPTHS

While sitting in the passenger's seat, I looked over my shoulder and saw the boys home van approach. Pops and Betty pulled up and parked on the other side of the gas pump.

I was three feet away from being caught.

My heart started pounding, my knees got weak, and I knew I was done. As I laid the seat down in his Toyota Celica, I prayed. I prayed for a second chance. I prayed for a new life.

I needed this escape to happen.

I wanted a new start; I wanted a new life.

All that blocked my certain capture was a single gas pump. I could hear them talking about me as they pumped gas and chain smoked. They were upset and determined to catch me.

Pops called me every name in the book and talked about what the men in there would do to me. He did not know I could hear every word he uttered. I was helpless and as good as caught.

As we pulled away, I could not believe how close of a call that was.

But I had escaped.

Now, what was the next step?

- Do I sell marijuana again?
- Do I join my other aunt's crew in Long Beach making and selling crystal meth?
- Do I even have a next step?
- Will I be homeless again?
- Should I end my own worthless life?

The Bright Lights Call Me Again

My head was spinning with all the possibilities. I could not turn myself in unless I wanted to be locked up until 18, if I even made it that long in there.

When David came back to town, I met up with him and his mother. They were heading to Las Vegas to visit his grandparents.

It was a weekend journey that would change my fortune and finally give me hope.

My grandparents were also there. So, I asked if I could tag along. It was harboring a fugitive, but they agreed. They knew that I needed to figure out the next step in life and gave me an escape for a weekend.

This was a way out of California with escorts.

Once we arrived in Las Vegas and met with my Gma, things would forever change.

My life would be given that small glimmer of hope that I was always searching for.

GMA SURPRISINGLY TAKES US IN

Gma

My Gma was always distant toward my mother and our whole side of the family. We were the outcasts. We had nothing to offer her.

My mother resented and hated Gma for this. She always felt abandoned. They'd bicker at Christmas parties at my grandparents' house.

My mother even told me she walked in on my Gma having sex with one of my mom's ex-boyfriends.

(Not one to break a terrible cycle, my mother would continue the cruel tradition by sleeping with Melissa's husband later our story, and I would be the one to witness it.)

But my Gma certainly had a mind of her own, and it was her way or the highway.

She was an alcoholic bartender who always worked multiple jobs. Her raspy cigarette smoking voice still rings out in my head to this day. She had her favorites, and I surely was not one of them.

I remember one Christmas she bought my cousin a big stereo system and I got a walkman. Not even one with a cassette player.

I can think of a hundred different instances similar to this. I had so much resentment toward her. It almost bordered on hatred.

A Fresh Start

But it all changed the moment we reunited. She went from being someone who had nothing to do with me, to my hero. She gave me a big hug when we arrived and said, "I want to give you a chance in life. You are staying here with us."

That came straight out of left field.

I did not have any idea that I would be gifted such an amazing opportunity. I never believed my Gma loved us and learned to resent her over the years. Yet here we were, at a critical time in my life, and she became my champion. I felt loved and wanted at a very low moment.

My grandparents had a beautiful home. Flush with arcade games and pinball machines from the bar they had in California. They had a gorgeous pool with a waterfall and an island. They had an indoor and outdoor spa and all other amenities. This home was huge.

I went from being a trailer park kid, abandoned and locked up, to living the dream life!

All I could think was, "Pinch me!" and, "Am I dreaming?" If so, please never wake me up from this incredible dream.

My Gma was old school and no-nonsense. I needed it. I never had structure in my life of any kind until the boys home.

Now I would use this time to learn to become a man. I wanted to be a better person.

My grandparents bought me second-hand clothes from the Goodwill that might have been a little tight, but, hey, I was in heaven. I would have worn anything they asked for this new chance at life.

I had had no place in the world. But now I did. I was given my first real chance, and I felt loved and wanted.

My Gma made a phone call to my parole officer and requested custody of me. I was all of 15 years old with a very checkered past. But how could the same woman who abandoned her own children be my champion?

She left three of her kids on my aunt's doorstep and never took custody of them again. But now she was going to take me in? How could she go from being so self-centered and standoffish to my hero?

How could a lady who turned her back and ran from any conflict choose to do this for me?

I had heard so many horror stories that I did not know what to believe. And, to this day, I do not know what brought it out in her. The kindness, the caring, the opportunity she presented was more than I could have ever hoped for. It was also more than I deserved.

I would soon let her and my grandfather down, but we will discuss that more soon.

My Gma was an angel to me. Her wings spread out and they sheltered me. She protected me. I was held in her warm embrace and had no worries in the world. She was my angel even if her halo had cracks and was held together with super glue. She was mine.

For that short period in my life, I felt invincible. I was the wanted. I was the loved.

When I had hit depths of depression that I was scared I would not pull out of, she was there for me. I contemplated suicide on so many occasions. I was a very emotional child, and that carried over into my teen years.

I was a loner of sorts like I had been throughout all my childhood. I had a hard time communicating with people and was very shy unless I was trying to sell something to earn money. I would walk on the opposite side of the street when I saw a pretty girl coming toward me.

My Gma taught me so much in the eight months I lived with them. She taught me about responsibility, humility, and honoring my word. She aided me to be the best person I could possibly be. She was hard on me in a good way. She would speak her mind but refused to cuss.

I miss her each and every single day.

She had a 1950s-style beehive hairdo long after anyone else. Her red hair always stood out in a crowd. Her voice was always raspy from all the cigarettes and alcohol. She was as damaged as we all were. But she was mine, and she looked out for me.

She went through a string of men just like my mother did. I am sure you can see the pattern.

She had broken marriages, multiple fathers for her children, and a very addictive personality.

She loved to drink, smoke, and gamble. It was a daily cycle.

She would get up around 4:00 to 4:30 AM every morning and do her hair and makeup. Other than when she was in the hospital, I never saw her without either done. She was very outgoing, a bartender by trade. She was exactly what I needed at this stage of my life.

I still wonder where I would have ended up without her guidance. I am sure I would have been in prison or ended up dead.

New Structure and Rules

My Gma had this sense about her. She would never shy away from anything or anyone. No argument was won against her.

She ruled the roost, and you did what she asked, or else.

I had never had any kind of structure in my life before now. I had a curfew. I was allotted half an hour a day on the phone, tops. I had chores to do. I was also required to get back into high school.

My freshman year of high school back in California was plagued with torture in the boys home, escapes, and way too many absences. This would not be allowed on my Gma's watch.

I was expected to finish high school, go to college, and make something of my life. That was a lot of pressure, and I was used to making easy money. I was used to seeing people hustle for whatever they wanted.

What was work?

That seemed like a bad word of sorts to me. I needed to retrain my whole thought process. I needed to learn how to be a man. I needed to learn that our actions define who we are. Our lives are our own.

Easy money comes and goes much too quickly. But to have structure and to work toward achieving your goals is priceless. Earning your money makes you have respect for it and for yourself.

Sometimes growing up is much harder than being homeless though. You need to find yourself and build a different mindset. It's a shift when you are used to coming and going as you please, never having to answer to anyone or explain yourself. I was used to getting away with anything I wanted.

This life of structure and expectations was tough.

I believe, without role models, most teenagers are lost. I also believe my generation is littered with lost souls who never had someone to look up to, emulate, or strive to be like. They have a hard uphill climb all alone.

I know people claim that being a product of your environment does not exist or is an excuse, but I strongly disagree.

Those who say that have never:
- Been jumped by a gang
- Been beaten bloody for having a different color of skin or for walking on the wrong side of the street
- Had people follow them through stores because you looked grungy, so they assumed you were a thief
- Felt what it's like to starve
- Slept out on the cold streets, homeless

Racism comes in many forms, many colors. And when it does come, it hits you like a freight train. I have both physical and mental scars that I will take with me to my grave.

Those of us who can survive the tough environment can become leaders. We can share our life experiences to make a positive change in this world.

Sometimes decisions are forged from necessity, not want. Sometimes we are not dealt the same cards as others. Sometimes our pain is hidden behind blue eyes in deep depths.

Do not look at life's trials as a weakness. Use this as your strength. You lived through hell. Now, you can forge a path out of it. You use this newfound structure to build your path to a better future.

So many people do not understand this and don't realize that they can use hard moments for positive growth. Gangs are an escape from an even more uncertain future for some. They could be death for others.

For me, to go from hell to paradise was something I had a hard time adjusting to.

My Gma was a diligent worker and had two to three jobs at a time. She had strict rules that needed to be followed. If I were to make this work I needed to do a 180-degree turn and change my entire mindset.

I needed to retrain myself. I wish it was something I could have learned overnight. But I was too stubborn and wild back then.

Although I wished back then that I was stronger, now I am glad I was not. The life lessons I learned from being weak have served me well in my later years. My life would have been different.

Melissa Comes to Vegas Too

My Gma decided to take a chance on my little sister in her home as well. But even at only 13, Melissa was much harder than I was. She was tough as tough could be. She had been through so much more, so this was an even bigger culture shock to her than it ever was to me.

We were both given a chance, but my sister and Gma were both very strong-willed, hard headed, and stubborn beyond belief. With this, our time together was always a constant struggle and short-lived.

Melissa grew up on the streets even more so than I had. Gma would ask her to do something, and she would rebel.

She suffered all kinds of abuse but believed she was still in control. Or, at least, she wanted to be in control.

Melissa had stopped going to school regularly when she was only 10 years old, and it showed. She would come up with off the wall comments that made no sense whatsoever. She almost talked in gibberish at times.

I felt for her because she only got to see the bad in people.

Her life was built on negativity, and that is a battle she fights to this very day. She is a tormented soul who reminds me so much of our mother.

School was never important in our household. It was more important to eat, make money, or be the showpieces in money acquisition scams for our mother and her evil crew. Melissa had already met her first love and longed to be back in California and in his arms.

So, she would steal money out of our grandparents' jukebox or video games and call him from pay phones. When my Gma caught on to what she was doing, Melissa was gone.

She left the life of luxury we were offered to run the streets again.

She gave up paradise for freedom. She ran from a good thing.

Looking back, we were uncontrollable, just like the courts had said. We were lost kids trying to find a glimmer of love and hope. We always looked for more and always seemed to end up with so much less.

So my little sister hopped on a bus back to California to start her life with her first love. Not too long afterward, she became pregnant with Vanessa, her first of five children.

Another case of children having children. She was just 14 when she got pregnant and had my first niece at 15 years old.

My time at my Gma's was not going much smoother for me either. Yes, I wanted the life that had been laid in front of me, but I would not listen and didn't think I deserved good things.

I felt that I had not earned the right to this new world but was too lazy to prove myself.

MORE MISTAKES, TIME TO FLY

Old Habits Die Hard

As you saw, I did not do well with structure. I was still uncontrollable.

I had been so used to easy money and hustling that when the real world came calling, I turned my cheek. By this time I had made a few friends on the street where my grandparents and I lived.

We started going to church every Sunday. I had only been in churches in the past to get money for my mother, so this was much different. They had youth groups, and we all had a blast. I started to find my place in this new town.

I was going to be a good kid and make a difference.

My best friend David had gone back to Palmdale after our first weekend in Las Vegas, but we always kept in touch, and about three months later he moved to Las Vegas with his mother and two brothers. We were inseparable; we were best friends. We went to the same high school and had classes together. We were best friends across two states now.

We are even friends to this very day.

School was trying because people were so much different in Las Vegas than they were in California. I had only a few friends and always had to fight for what I felt was respect. One day three kids said that I needed to move from my seat.

I asked, "Why?"

They said, "It's our seat, and if you do not move, you will get your ass kicked."

The teacher was not in the room yet, so I kicked my shoes off and said, "Let's go."

They asked if I knew Karate.

I said, "I know one thing, and that is I will kick each and every one of your asses." I did not plan on being bullied at this school. I stood my ground.

I had started to build my reputation. Another guy picked a fight with me earlier, and I threw him across the desk. I had fight after fight. My Gma was getting frustrated, and my grandfather was beginning to resent me. I had a hard time in this new school.

The coach even threw me up against the wall and said he would teach me a lesson because I was playing football too rough for the other kids.

My Crew of Chaos

During this time I became a part of a group of friends who did not have a conscience. Our crew went around tormenting the whole city.

We would cruise Las Vegas Boulevard at night in mini trucks and Volkswagen bugs and cause havoc and grief.

Our friends had the vehicles, and we were there for the fights and for the girls. I regret how much of a jerk I was at that time in my life. Some of the things I did disgust me.

I was a broken teenager who wanted to rebel against the world. I found ways of doing so at innocent people's expense.

The theme of writing this book is that we all make mistakes. We can all be lost, unloved, unwanted. But we need to use those times in life to grow. We grow even when we least expect it.

Every trial gives you a chance to reflect and grow, to help others too. It is up to us to see these opportunities and own them.

We did so many atrocious things. Here are several that I am not very proud of:
- We threw pizza at pedestrians.
- We threw sodas at people in suits. (Because we saw them as authority figures and were there to 'show them.')
- We picked fights with groups of people and had no remorse at the pain caused.

Las Vegas was a different world back then. Teenagers ruled the Strip with loudspeakers and heavy attitudes. Fists were always thrown, and the girls were always there to witness it all.

One time we were all cruising the Strip when a group of bodybuilders pulled up and ripped the antenna off of my friend Jared's car. We all got out of our vehicles. It was an all-out brawl. Fists flew, people were kicked, and others were chased.

We had eight of us, and they had five of them. I saw a couple of my friends get knocked to the ground. The biggest guy put me in a headlock. I kept punching him in the kidneys. He ripped a patch of my hair out, and I was furious.

My biggest insecurities were my receding hairline and my crooked teeth. I saw my hair fall to the ground, so I punched him in the nose and broke it. He ran, and I chased him. I kept kicking him in the ass.

Afterwards I was approached by a gang that asked me if I was interested in joining them. I said, "No." I was about the girls, not the fights.

This was a time for growth, in a way.

First Love

I had always revolved around the gang setting but wanted to be better for once.

Plus, there were so many pretty church girls who wanted nothing more than to piss off their parents by bringing a bad boy home.

I dated a few of them, but then I met one who stole my heart.

I constantly wrote her poetry, learned manners, and wanted to show her I was more. I wanted to be more for her. She was a lovely girl with bright blue eyes, an infectious smile, and a great demeanor.

Her name was April.

She was in a private Christian school, and I was her bad boy. I was the one who her parents would shake their heads at when they heard my name.

We promised each other the world. Our hearts, our virginity, and our eternal love.

I wrote my first poem to her:

> Cherish always as I do few.
> This is a rose I dedicate to you.
> As you and the rose have beauty to be found.
> One such a beauty, it is world renowned.
> Another a beauty that is seen by me.
> As always, my beauty, it is found in Thee.

With so much love in my heart, I was still a lost kid who fought structure. And I was about to throw a party that would send me back on the streets.

And I deserved it.

The Party

When David and I were back in Palmdale, we had a group of rich friends we idolized. They were the most popular guys in school, and we wanted to ride their coattails back then.

We could never have what they had. They were born with silver spoons. By contrast, David's nickname was "Re-wear" because he only had two pairs of pants that were exactly the same.

The popular kids always made sure they would rub that in. These guys ran the school and had all the girls they wanted. They were who we wanted to be. They had nice clothes, beautiful girls, fast cars, and loads of money.

Money was a prerequisite to being a part of this group. Money was something neither David nor I had. My grandparents told me when our friends (or so-called friends) came to Las Vegas they could stay in our home.

FROM THE DEPTHS

My fortune was about to change.

My grandparents had to leave town for a funeral, and my rich California friends called to say they were in Las Vegas and wanted to crash at my place.

At the time, I felt like I had something to prove. I would show them that they were no better than me. That they did not even have as much as I had. I lived on over an acre of land now.

My grandparents had even bought me a car, and it was covered up in the backyard behind the pool. After my grandparents left, I decided to peek at the car. It was exactly what I wanted: a Honda CRX SI.

This was my dream car at the time. I had the girl, the home, and they were going to pay for my schooling too. I could not believe they had listened and bought me the car of my dreams.

I would show these guys when they arrived that I was on their level now. They were no better than David or me.

But once they got there, all hell broke loose for the whole weekend. People were sniffing paint and huffing Freon. People were drinking alcohol and smoking weed. It was all out anarchy.

My grandparents' bar was on full display and bottles were disappearing faster than you can believe.

Skinny dipping was a prerequisite to join the party. We had naked people jumping into the pool and running through the house.

The island was littered with beer cans and bottles of booze. It was wild, and it was wrong. I was showing off but destroying whatever goodwill I had from my grandparents.

My grandfather was burying his mother, and I was throwing a party in his house.

I look back on this as a turning point in my life. I had thrown little parties when they were asleep before, but this was a whole new world. This was full-blown anarchy. As the weekend came to an end, so did the life I was trying to live.

Because of this party, I lost the love of my grandfather. I can say from the bottom of my heart that this was not my intention. But, it was my choice, and I will forever live with regret.

For this, I am sorry Richard. I am sorry I let you and Gma down.

I am sorry I was an immature kid, pretending to know who or what I was. I deserved to be thrown out and am man enough to look back with total regret and even gratitude.

At the time, I was an imposter trying to act as if I belonged. I did not deserve or earn the life I was trying to show off. I was simply along for the ride. And I threw away the very life I always wanted. I was just too stupid or oblivious to realize it yet.

While I was cleaning up vomit, pouring water in the vodka bottles, and trying to figure out how to rehang the curtains that had been ripped off the window, I was unaware that my grandparents came back a day early.

My girlfriend tried to warn me but to no avail. I had a mind of my own and would do what I wanted when I wanted to do it. I was living in a fantasy world that would soon alter course.

Once the front door opened, my life forever changed, again.

The time for reckoning was upon me.

It All Crumbles

My Gma cursed for the first time in my life, and I lost whatever love my grandfather had ever had for me. He hated me after this moment. He hates me to this very day. I cannot blame him and deserved every bit of it. I was young and cruel, and I was again unwanted and unloved.

But this time I earned every bit of that moniker.

The car in the backyard disappeared days later. All of the college money I had thought was there was now taken off of the table. I got the cold shoulder, yet deserved so much more. I deserved to be thrown out on my ass at that very moment.

I knew I was unwelcome and needed to figure out my next step.

April broke up with me and got together with someone I disliked from school. He and I would end up being pulled apart for throwing punches at church.

This guy was big and a part of a crew, a gang of sorts, that called themselves the Four Horsemen, part of a gang known as the Drifters.

On steroids, they played on every sports team and were all-state wrestlers.

April's new boyfriend was handsome, had a good head on his shoulders, and did not like me or what I stood for. Looking back now I see his point, but at that time in my life, he was enemy number one in my eyes.

He had taken the girl I had wanted to spend my life with. He had taken from me the only person who knew I was a virgin.

Was he the enemy? Or was I enemy number one? Was I the cause for all the strife in my life?

He and I bumped into one another in the mall not too long after they started dating. He was with her, and I was with my friend Lee. I mouthed off to him until he got into my face. I froze. This guy actually scared me.

This was an unfamiliar feeling, one I had not experienced since I escaped the boys home. Once he turned around, I mouthed off again. I called him a bitch to save face. You could see the anger forming, so he swung at me, and I ducked it and poked him in the forehead and said, "I could have knocked you out."

I was scared and had a can of mace in my jacket. Lee held my jacket and security came in to separate us before we could fight.

My grandparents were already trying to figure out how to tell me that I needed to move out when he and the other Four Horsemen showed up at my grandparents' front step.

I opened the door, and he said, "Come out so I can kick your ass."

I closed the door and turned to my Gma and told her I was scared and that I was going to get my ass kicked.

She said, "Stop being a pussy and go fight him one-on-one like a man."

I opened the front door and requested for the other three stooges to sit in the car while he and I fought. They listened, and I walked out to fight.

I punched him as hard as I could right on the button. I thought for sure he would go down. Boy, was I ever wrong.

He looked me dead in the eyes and said, "Oh, baby, that's what I like."

Just then the other three guys jumped the wall and ran toward me. I ran back into my grandparents' house, and they all followed me in, fists balled up to pummel me in my own home.

Whatever goodwill I had with my grandparents ended at this exact moment.

My Gma put a rifle up to the first guy's head and called him a pussy too.

She said, "Hey, Pussy, why couldn't you give my grandson a one-on-one fight? I have a bullet for you, you pussy!"

My Gma was a strong woman, but I never could have imagined this. She was no-nonsense, but I had long worn out my welcome.

I was causing a strain on her marriage, and it was time for me to go.

16 YEARS OLD: ON MY OWN

Help from a Friend or Two

Leaving my grandparents' place, I knew that I earned a pass back onto park benches, not knowing where my next meal or shower would come from.

My first thought was to go to a friend's house where my buddy David was already staying. It was his girlfriend Tricia and her mother Ann's home. Tricia was the first girl I had met in Las Vegas. We had become pen pals when she was out of town and flirted a lot until we met in person and realized we were more like brother and sister than lovers.

She worked at Circus Circus, along with David and a few other friends. I got a job there as well. We were all making a good paycheck and stealing money too.

I would buy a pack of Big Red gum and every time I took out a piece, I would drop a $20 bill into my pocket. So every day at work I would take home an extra $100. I am not proud of being a thief back then.

These were times that I struggled in my own skin.

These were the times that helped me forge a good work ethic. I was in between a hustler and a worker, but my lessons learned would set me down the right path eventually. I did everything wrong then, just to learn and know how to do everything right, now.

In my area of the casino, I made sure to be loud and try to attract more players. I would yell out, "We have a winner here!" And it worked. I was even recognized for making more than the game's average on 15 out of my last 16 days. It was a blast.

We all had the time of our childhood back then. I even saw friends from California when they would show up at Circus Circus. One girl who I had a crush on back in California, but would never give me the time of day, flirted with me and I felt like I had conquered the world.

Most of us workers were let go before 90 days were up because they did not want to give us health insurance or any benefits. So with the money we all saved up, we got our first apartment.

Short-Lived Independence

It was a terrific 2-bedroom apartment that had a gazebo and waterfalls throughout the property. We had done well with stashing money, and this was our reward. We often hosted parties, and all the high school girls loved us. With no rules, we were an escape.

I was still just 16 years old.

I would crash out with three or four girls on my bed, but I was always respectful. I was still a virgin, yet no one knew. Not even David knew. The only person who did know this fact, April, had just lost her virginity to my now enemy. I was destroyed.

It all started getting too real because of the other guys who would show up at all of the parties.

One day a friend ended up at the apartment with four other guys and no girls, so I asked them to leave. He flashed a gun, and when I saw the gun his friend jumped in front of him, and I punched him in the face. His head left an imprint in the wall. Then my friend threw him down the front steps on the second floor.

I called out the guy with the gun and said we needed to settle this with fists. He said that he would and asked if he could tie his shoes. I let him and paid for it. His friend yelled my name, and then I was bum rushed.

He threw me on a van and punched me in the nose so hard that it knocked me out. I did not fall; I was knocked out of my senses but was still standing. I came to with him punching me in my ribs and on my sides.

When I regained awareness, I flipped him over my leg onto his back and kept punching him in the face until they pulled me off. He had ring prints all over. My blood was everywhere.

He lost the fight, but I looked so much worse because of a broken nose.

As they picked him up off of the floor, I asked if he were ready for round two and the loser would pay for lunch.

We both laughed, went into the house, and cleaned ourselves up.

We only had that apartment for a few months before both David and I ended up moving into his girlfriend's house.

17 YEARS OLD: LEAVING LAS VEGAS

17 Years Old

Tricia's mom Ann was a kind-hearted lady who looked out for all us kids in the neighborhood.

She was a cocktail waitress with big green eyes and long red hair. She and her daughter were always there for us to talk to and to confide in.

Ann taught us to drive and let us borrow her car to go to the drive-in movies. Those of us with no money would hide in the trunk to get in for free.

We would do crazy things like hang out of the car and try to touch our fingertips to the ground while driving.

We felt alive.

Losing My Virginity

I had dated many girls but was old-fashioned and longed to fall in love and be with one person for the rest of our lives.

I thought I had found that but got a rude wake-up call because of my many mistakes during those years. I had found April but pushed her away.

Now, as I was about to turn 17, a beautiful girl was very persistent and rode her bike across town to spend quality time with me while no one was home. That would be the day I lost my virginity. All of three minutes of shame on the living room floor.

I had planned for so long in my mind how this would happen and with whom, that when it did happen I froze and became an asshole.

I asked her to leave because people would be coming home soon. She had big blue eyes, a slender build, and was just in the Teen Nevada pageant.

She was kind but naïve, and I had just used her. I did not love her and knew that nothing more could come of this. I took advantage of this sweet girl.

I was disgusted with myself and who I was becoming.

How could I be this person? I didn't even want to look at myself in the mirror. The reflection that looked back was nothing more than a hollow teenager lost in his own imaginary world.

Hawaii Calling

During this time my mother had kicked the drugs and moved to Maui, Hawaii with her sister Jennifer and her beautiful family. She had Melissa and my niece Vanessa move out there with her too.

Melissa and our mother worked on the pineapple farms picking pineapples. They would come home with bloody hands and tell me stories of huge spiders and other disgusting insects.

They worked their butts off, and quickly my sister got homesick and went back to her baby's father Ringo back home in California.

My mother felt alone, so she asked if I wanted to move to Maui with her. She said I would not have to go to school, just work for her boyfriend. I decided this was my next move.

I would move to paradise and start a new life. So, she bought me a one-way ticket a month out.

In my sophomore year, I dropped out of school and never looked back. I wish I had a good high school experience, as I feel it is paramount to a child's growth into adulthood. I was much too lazy and fixated on other things, so my schoolwork became secondary.

And as I prepared to leave, I ignored the poor girl who took my virginity. She was crushed, and I was a monster. I think I had a complex that I wanted to hurt the world for all the pain I had experienced.

It took years of therapy to realize the hate I harbored for myself was what I threw out to the world, and she was a victim. I blamed her for taking my virginity when she had no clue I was a virgin. She didn't deserve my being such a jerk.

The one thing that I can tell you about writing a book is you see your life differently in retrospect.

You can see how many mistakes you made along the way. And the great part is how you see those mistakes were actually guiding you on your path to growth and enlightenment, even though you couldn't see it at the time. They stay with you on this journey called life and help you to become a better person.

None of us are perfect. It is all a journey.

Jimmy Colson

My Last Days in Vegas

I knew my days were numbered in Las Vegas, so I chose to live life to the fullest. We went cliff diving with 20 to 30 people at a time in Lake Mead. We would get drunk, party, and escape reality for a few hours.

I remember right before I left we got into a rumble. We had probably 40 to 50 people fighting in all.

A girl from our party decided to grab a girl from a rival high school by the hair and beat her up. As she punched her in the face repeatedly, all hell broke loose.

I chose who I was going to fight, put a rock in my hand, and busted his head open. Blood was everywhere. He started to cry.

"Look what you did to me," I said to him. "Tell me you are a pussy."

I beat him more until he screamed, "I am a pussy! I am a pussy!"

Writing this disgusts me now. I do not know how I found humor or any kind of validation in being a bad person. I was not a good person at this point in my life.

I was not a lost kid — I was a villain. I was a bully and an abuser.

I hurt girls' feelings, and guys had scars when they crossed my path. I was a menace. I was lost in my own mind. I had no business thinking I was anything more than a thug. I wanted to show the world who I was, and as I look back, I disgust myself.

I was nothing more than a bad kid who wanted to pretend he was something more.

I use this time in my life as a reflection of the sub-person I was to better myself now. For all the pain I caused then, I want to help others aid in healing now.

My time in Las Vegas had come to an end.

I was nothing more than a tyrant who liked to inflict pain because I could not escape my own. I wanted to hurt the world as it had hurt me.

I had a sickness and no cure. I needed an escape, and it came in the form of my mother wanting to make amends.

Or so I thought.

HAWAII

Getting to Work

My mother had been a part of the drug scene in California for close to 20 years. She morphed from a great mommy into Satan right before our very eyes.

Now, would a fresh start in Hawaii be a recipe for all I wanted in a relationship with her?

Well, not long after that my mother asked me to move in, she shacked up with the manager of an International House of Pancakes, and they loved to drink themselves into drunken stupors every single night.

His name was Mark.

He had the whole dork thing down to a tee. He had glasses, a receding hairline, and a squeaky little voice. He was no more than a buck thirty soaking wet.

Mark was the opposite of what my mother looked for in men and exactly what she needed at this point in her life. He was management, so he got me a job at both stores on the island. I would put in eight hours at one IHOP, and then they would ship me to the other one to put in six to eight more hours bussing the tables there too.

Fights Still Follow Me

Life was not easy in Hawaii because local Islanders would pick fights with me for no reason. At least, I felt like they did not have a reason, but they believed we took their island, jobs, land, and hearts. They had a point.

I even got into a fight with a guy from a gang called the Maui Boyz. I threw him down after he hit me and got a few good swings in on him. He warned me that my time would come.

Hawaii back in the 90s was a different world. The Islanders did not like us ruining their land. We were outsiders and minorities. We were unwanted and unwelcome. He said he would not forget me and he did not.

I also did demolition work and helped my Aunt Jennifer hang drapes for her company. Although I was living in a beautiful paradise, I was always working.

I went from being on the streets to living in one of the most desired places in the world. But at what cost?

I was very homesick, and the Islanders did not take kindly to "Haoles" or "Howlies," as they called us.

We were living in a Section 8 Housing complex called Harbor Lights. Most people there were on Welfare, or they were Islanders who could no longer afford their homes and were driven into these cookie-cutter, small apartments. The animosity and anger shined through.

I was 17 and being blonde haired and blue eyed made me a devil to them. They would razz me, chase me, and throw things at me. It was an interesting life, to say the least.

One day I met this pretty local girl. We were talking about Las Vegas, Maui, and life in general. I heard from the third floor, "You no like talk to my sista or you like beef with me."

I had no idea what "beef with me" meant until three huge Islanders came running after me.

I ran fast, but they were actually catching up to me. I got in the elevator and prayed. The door shut right before they stomped me into the ground. Check 'narrowly escaping the ass-kicking of my life' off my bucket list.

The Beauty

I did make a couple friends though. One was a Disc Jockey at the radio station and another great friend was an Islander named Kaleo.

He was awesome, and people loved and respected him. He always made sure I did not get my ass kicked, always had a joint rolled, and was good for constant laughs. Kaleo is still my friend to this very day.

A big guy, probably pushing 300 pounds, but he could kick over his head. We would have long talks about life, spirituality, and the Island. The Island was now a love of mine. The crystal blue waters, the green mountain tops, black sand beaches, and the Seven Sacred Pools.

Hana means heaven in Hawaiian.

I truly believe that this is as close as you can come to heaven on Earth. The ocean breeze blowing across your brow. The hint of saltwater even when you are inland. The lush vegetation. All the colors of the flowers and the vines and trees so green that they look unreal.

One day I decided to write a poem about the most charming place I had ever set my eyes upon.

FROM THE DEPTHS

> Hana...
> This is the place of dreams.
> The waterfalls crash as the birds sing.
> A beautiful melody.
> In this enchanting place by the sea.
> The water like glass from an angel's tears.
> The beauty has alas lasted all these years.
> The vines live as life has the touch.
> The water arrives as it does such.
> A beautiful dance as it crashes down.
> On this calm, beautiful, glorious ground.
> This place is one and yes you can.
> Live in peace on the hot Maui sand.

Those initial experiences on Maui helped shape me for the future. I learned to love the world and to look at the beauty we are surrounded by. I learned that I wanted to have class, not just money. I wanted to make a difference and discovered that I was drawn to the ocean.

Looking up from the dark depths, I could see life and vibrancy.

I learned that life is more than what meets the eye. Life is intricate, life is marvelous. The ocean calls out to me every day. Even today. I love all of the fish of the sea, the corals, the movement as the corals sway back and forth doing their beautiful dance.

The colors are out of this world. Sea turtles are always there to say hello.

This is truly my heaven and where my ashes will rejoin my family in the ocean at Black Rock in Kaanapali. My Gma's ashes were left there first, followed by my mother's and stepfather's too.

Now they are all a part of the beauty to take in there. I feel their spirits as I snorkel. I know they are still with us and writing this makes me think back to my childhood…to actually remember the good times when I was younger…

But, I digress. Let's get back on track with the story again.

More Drama

Maui was stunning, but it took a toll on me. I was lonely. My cousin Michele was my best friend there and my confidant. She was 15 and has always been there for me. She has a lovely soul.

One day she took me to a UB40 concert. It was the third concert I had ever attended. It was in an open air stadium.

The smell of marijuana and BBQ was everywhere. Locals sang along.

It was an amazing experience, or so I thought.

The next thing I knew, a group of gang members from the Maui Boyz appeared and started a little game called "Beat Down the Howlies."

They found every white person there and started punching them. They all danced around like a mosh pit, throwing fists, and kicking away. The guy I fought inside IHOP spotted me and said, "There is da Howlie!"

I ran. I ran so fast and hid. I knew my days were numbered if they got ahold of me.

Dreaming of Las Vegas

I left the concert and didn't look back.

I was now nervous to go to work, I was nervous to leave the apartment, and I was homesick. I kept in touch with friends back in Las Vegas. David had moved to West Virginia while I was in Maui but his girlfriend Tricia was one of my closest friends.

And the first friend I had made in Las Vegas, Anthony, was still there.

My 18th birthday was fast approaching.

Every day was the same. I worked 12 to 16 hours, slept, and then went back to work.

I was able to save a few thousand dollars, so I felt I could maybe go back to Las Vegas and find an apartment.

I bought a gold nugget ring and a leather jacket.

I was learning to respect myself.

PART 5

BECOMING AN ADULT

Jimmy Colson

18TH BIRTHDAY TRAUMA

Another Cage

The day of my 18th birthday was also my mother's 37th birthday. I was hoping to talk with her about my thoughts on going back to Las Vegas.

However, when I arrived home, she and her friend were shit-faced drunk, slurring their words and yelling at me.

I confronted my mom, reminding her that she had promised to stay sober to celebrate our birthdays together.

In response, she slammed down her empty gallon of vodka, and she and her friend jumped me.

They beat my ass. I did not swing back; I just kept mouthing off.

"Keep hitting me, you old drunk bitches!"

They were sloppily swinging away. That helped me make up my mind. I would catch a flight back to Las Vegas and be with my friends again.

I knew that the ocean would still call for me, but this island became a cage. Another cage I needed to break out from. Another prison of the mind.

I could not walk outside my apartment because I feared being beaten up.

I could not go to work without worrying about the same.

And, yet again, I could not trust or rely on my mother.

I knew that I could no longer try to call this magical island home. I would escape this paradise and create my own.

Going Away Party Torture

Kaleo and my friend Esa had a going away party for me, and I got trashed.

They brought this beautiful Island girl with them to say goodbye. She was half Japanese and a lot of fun.

But then, she pulled off my pants in front of everyone and decided to have intercourse with me.

I kept saying, "No!" but my friends held me down.

She rode me, and I had no choice. I was innocent at that time, as I had only had sex once in my life.

I was embarrassed and ashamed.

I was so lost and hurt.

I was still in love with my first crush April but had now had sex with two other women. April and I had promised each other our virginity. She had found the love of her life (they are still married to this very day), but I was not over her.

I was teased pretty relentlessly by my friends before I left for Sin City.

BACK TO LAS VEGAS

A New Start

I boarded the flight back to Las Vegas with a pocket full of cash and a purpose. I would make a life for myself. I had learned how to work. I had learned how to love myself.

When I landed, I got a big hug from Tricia. It was the first contact with someone I cared about in almost a year. I did not want to let her go.

She was my best friend's girlfriend, but if she hadn't been, I would have tried to make her my own. I was lost and lonely, and she was beautiful. She had the sweetest voice and was broken in ways like I was.

I went back with Tricia to her mother Ann's house. They let me crash out on their couch. Ann was a saint for all she did for us teenagers. Such a huge heart. She always put a smile on our faces. She was an awesome person and very pretty.

Ann always helped us kids and never expected anything in return. I saw her a few years ago, and all I could do was hug her and thank her. Thank her for seeing something more in me than I saw in myself. Thank her for caring enough to help me believe in myself.

Back with My Friends

My friend Anthony told me that his mother (who lived across the street from my grandparents) would let me stay with them, so I headed over there.

FROM THE DEPTHS

When I got to Anthony's house, his mom said that she had never agreed to my moving in, but she would let me stay there for a few weeks.

I was so vain that I would sleep with a baseball cap on my head to hide the fact that my hairline was receding more and more each day. In the morning, I would spend an hour doing the little bit of hair I had only to throw a cap over most of it.

David was moving back from West Virginia, so we contacted his mom, and she said I could live with them for $400 a month in a shared room. David and I each would take a bunk on the bunk beds, and David's brother Brady would sleep on a full-sized bed in the same room. It was right in the heart of the trailer park.

David and I were always listening to Depeche Mode, feeling moody, and sulking around depressed. His mom acted as if I were her best friend and was always mad at her three sons.

She would take me to spiritual bookstores, read my tarot cards, and all around make me feel important.

I never had self-worth, but she told me how handsome I was and that I should be a model. This build-up could only last so long. She and David had a fight, and she threw us both out. I had paid her six months rent upfront, and now I found myself homeless just a couple of months back into town.

Back on the streets, on park benches, and in abandoned apartments, friends' backyards, or closets.

I had worked so hard for a start on life only to have my friend's bipolar, moody mom take advantage of me and snatch all of my money.

This was the same lady who had brought me to Las Vegas when I went AWOL from the boys home. The same lady who had built me up. Now, she left me dangling and wondering what to do next.

I traveled across the ocean from Maui to Las Vegas. Went from working too much to not having a job or a home. Went from the beauty of the sea to the stress of finding a place to lay my head at night.

It was a turning point. Or so, I thought.

Living in the city of lights can be stressful when you are trying to sleep. It is a 24-hour town, so people honk at you even when you were sleeping. They throw things at you, call you names, or even start fights to try to impress their friends.

It was the karma I deserved.

Needing to Change

Often I would sleep in my friend Steve's backyard or my friend Jay's closet. One day Jay's mother found me and threw shoes at me, yelling that I was not welcome and to never come back.

I had tried to better myself before, but this was the wake-up call I needed. I finally clearly saw that I needed to make changes.

Not just financially, but from within. Spiritually. I needed to live every day to the fullest. I had been a fool and decided I would no longer be one. I found a job at Albertsons bagging groceries.

I would stay up all night walking the streets and then go to my Gma's house once my grandfather went to work and take a nap.

She would wash my clothes. I did this every day for about four months.

Then I met a couple of other guys who found abandoned apartments to sleep in. People would move out and painters would go in to retouch the paint. They sometimes left the windows open behind them.

So, we'd go in and sleep. Sometimes, if we were lucky, they'd even leave beds behind.

One day I was sleeping on a bed in an abandoned apartment, while the other guys were playing with fire. They put cologne on their hands and lit it on fire. I awoke to see the bed that I was sleeping in on fire. I ran out of that apartment and never looked back.

That was such a frightening situation. I easily could have died.

Time to try something else.

I found a few co-workers who were looking for a roommate, and they welcomed me with open arms — five guys in a 3-bedroom apartment made for interesting times. Rent was cheap since we all split the bills and the one person who had the master bedroom paid a little more.

It was a great set up. I met a girl who worked at Burger King and even had my first girlfriend in a couple of years.

All things were finally pointing in the right direction. My girlfriend and I were intimate, and she was always happy and acted as if she cared. However, one day at a party these three guys came up to me and said, "Hey, are you dating Skittles?"

I asked, "Who?"

They said, "Skittles Kim."

I said, "Yes, Kim is my girlfriend but why do you call her Skittles?"

They said, "Man, you really don't know? Because all of us mother fuckers have fucked her. She has fucked more dudes than Skittles in a package."

I was crushed.

I could not believe the first real relationship I was in was with someone like her. I went to her window and started throwing rocks to get her attention while the other two guys hid around the corner. They told me they would lift up one of them to go in through her window to have sex.

She answered and asked me why I did not just go to the door. They came out from around the corner and confronted her. She broke into tears. She was caught and did not deny cheating with everyone in the neighborhood.

I believe I deserved this karma for what I had done before I left for Maui. I took someone's innocence, and now I got mine taken from me. I had not worn protection when we made love, so I was worried and got tested.

I prayed that nothing was wrong.

When my tests came back clean, I knew I needed to be safe. I needed to make sure I practiced safe sex. I was much too young for a child or to catch a sexually transmitted disease. I do not know what I would have done if I caught a disease or had gotten her pregnant.

About a week later, I bet you could not guess who had quit her job at Burger King and was now working with me at Albertsons? It was none other than Skittles herself.

She almost immediately started dating another coworker of ours. He did not have a clue about her and her very checkered past (and present). A month later, the two of them announced that she was pregnant with their first child. I was mortified. I was so scared that I might possibly be a father.

I felt for the child too. What if the child was not his?

I felt terrible for him, but I decided to keep my mouth shut. What was I to do? The child deserved to have a father. And he was a good guy. He heard about the skeletons in her closet but stood by her side through it all. I commend him and respect him for this.

Who was I to judge her? I had no idea of her past struggles or her insecurities or bouts of depression. We all have demons and skeletons. They aid us in growth too.

Two weeks later, when the rent was due for our apartment, one of my roommates decided to gamble the rent money. He was the roommate who had the lease in his name, so he was the one we gave our money to. He told us he was sorry and that he had gambled away every cent of our rent.

Here we go again.

Jimmy Colson

MEAN STREETS

Darkness

I had no money, no home to lay my head down in at night, and I was thrust back on the streets.

Again.

During this time I had been promoted to the bakery, so I had to be at work at 4 AM every day.

That worked out for me because I would sleep a couple of hours in the break room after walking the streets.

When I got off of work, my Gma would wash my clothes and let me take a nap in the motorhome in my grandparents' backyard.

Some days I overslept and had to sneak out so my grandfather didn't see me.

Times were tough.

I was able to save up some money since I didn't have rent to pay, but it took its toll on my mind and soul.

It was hard to live like this, going through the motions lonely every day. Walking around each and every night until I could take a nap was too much.

I had to find something else.

With thoughts of suicide, I was teetering.

FROM THE DEPTHS

I wrote this poem during one of the darkest of times:

> Can love and destiny begin to entwine?
> The doves, oh, can you see as they do fly?
> Flying high above the clouds as high as they can.
> But can they save the heart of this lonely man?
> I seek an angel for me to love.
> Yet hatred and deceit slap me from high above.
> Trying hard to let my feelings show.
> But totally unsure to let my love flow.
> Let it flow like the oceans, like the rivers,
> Like the seas so true.
> Why can I not find this angel I seek?
> I am blue with tears dripping from my eyes,
> Down my face.
> My heart skipping, no lies and no trace.
> Of this angel of my dreams.
> Only depression in the nights as I scream.
> A silent scream out of sight.
> It was only a dream in the middle of last night.

I knew life had to be better than this. With the money I had saved up, I had to find my place and was invited to move in with a previous roommate and two other friends.

After about a month, I saw one of these friends in front of the 7-Eleven as two guys started pushing him around.

His name was Tim.

Tim was about 6'2" with a very slender build. I would guess he was no more than 130 pounds soaking wet. He was a quiet kid, somewhat of a loner, and had no ill will towards anyone, or so I thought.

They were pushing Tim back and forth, taunting him, and calling him names. I asked these jerks to stop.

They asked me if I had a problem and if I wanted to fight them. I was somewhat of a hothead in those days and never backed away from a brawl.

I said to both of them, "If you give me a one-on-one, I'll fight either one of you."

Tim ran away in a flash. This guy looked like a track athlete with how fast he disappeared. I could not believe it. I went to protect him, and he left me with these two gang members to fight by myself.

I think he did it for self-preservation. However, back then that did not matter.

All that mattered was my preparing to fight these bullies. I had recognized both of them from a couple of years ago. We had gone to the same high school in Las Vegas. They were in the Drifters gang.

They always picked on kids, smacked them around, and took their money.

Now I was face to face with two all alone.

They said, "Let's do this."

I grabbed some mace in my pocket and sprayed it in the first guy's face and eyes. He fell to his knees.

I told the second guy, "Now we have a fair fight."

Then I broke his nose, kneed him in the face three times, and kicked him repeatedly. I went over to the guy I had sprayed with mace and kicked him a few times as well.

When I got back to the apartment, I let Tim know what I had done.

He was scared and warned me that I had opened up a can of worms that I would have to deal with. He wanted nothing of this fight, and it was now my cross to bear.

Ivy

I met another young lady during this time, Ivy. She was beautiful with blonde hair, big green eyes, and a smile that could stop traffic.

She was also innocent. She was a virgin and really cared about me.

Her father was a police officer who felt his daughter deserved someone better. Looking back now, I do not blame him. Back then, I did not see myself for who I actually was. Having a daughter of my own now has made me see the light.

One day while I was at work, Ivy's father showed up and almost started a fight with me, telling me to stay away from his daughter. He threatened to either beat me up or arrest me.

Despite the warning, we continued to see each other anyway, and when Ivy and her family went on a Caribbean cruise, she asked me to watch her stuffed animal that she slept with and to take it home with me, so that I would feel close to her.

She left this raggedy old bear with a ripped nose on the trampoline in her backyard, protected by her huge dog (also named Bear). I jumped the wall and Bear chased me.

I had to get two friends to climb over too and help until I was able to get the stuffed bear and bring it home. I cherished it because I knew she had had this stuffed animal her whole life and wanted me to hold it for her.

When she got back, I went to her house with my friend. Her mother was always very kind to me, but when we heard her father pull up, we hid. I heard him ask Ivy's brother, "Who is here?"

The brother replied, "Jimmy." He boomed, "Jimmy Colson?" and ran up the stairs to throw us out.

She and I talked for another couple of weeks or so until Valentine's Day. She brought me a box of candy, a stuffed animal, and a card saying how much she loved me, but that her father wanted her to break up with me.

I was crushed; this girl had my heart. I wrote poetry about her all of the time like this one:

> To you, I give my love, it is real.
> Nothing can explain the way I feel.
> To fall through the sky as light as a feather.
> To me, it is love and will last forever.
> To kiss you to hold you to feel good inside.
> There is no need to run and no need to hide.
> The feelings, the thoughts that go through my head.
> The path to destiny is the one that has led.
> Me to you, and you to me.
> Entangled in the arms of ecstasy.

Although heartbroken, I continued to work. However, I was threatened and fighting all the time. I needed protection.

At work one day, yet another guy named Greg started a fight with me. I told him, "I'll see you around." And when we bumped into each other at a bowling alley, my friend and I followed him and his girlfriend outside.

While standing behind his girlfriend, he sucker punched me in the ear. My ear rang. I said to her, "You need to go, or you are getting knocked out too."

She ran.

Greg and I threw punches but both missed. I threw a flying back fist and busted his eye open. Blood was everywhere.

He kept bouncing around, and security came after we each got a few shots off.

Greg and I are now friends to this day.

It is funny how altercations during childhood can turn into friendship and respect when we get older. I am glad we are friends. He is now a Judo instructor and has earned a black belt.

Another guy started a fight with me at Albertsons and brought out a baseball bat. I beat the heck out of him and threw his baseball bat at him as he ran off.

I could not believe how often I fought. Little did I know that the scuffle I had gotten into at 7-Eleven would soon come back to haunt me.

Brush with the Law

My newly ex-girlfriend Ivy knew the guys I had fought, and she had let it slip where I lived. She was also now dating one of their friends.

I came home with a note on my door staying that they would be back to kick my ass. It had 15 different signatures of people who wanted to destroy me. Now they knew who I was and where I lived.

I could not escape this any longer.

The guy, whose nose I broke, had had to go to the hospital. They were furious and wanted me to pay. They would take payment by beating me to a bloody pulp.

However, there was something they didn't know: I had recently bought a handgun.

It was a great-looking .38 Special Snub Nose. It was loaded with hollow tip bullets and snake shots. I would take it to work with me and leave it in my locker.

One day my friend's little brother stole it out of my locker and started shooting it up in the air at a house party.

The police showed up at my work, handcuffed me, and asked if I had ever seen the gun. I said that I had not. The officers told me they knew I was lying and would be able to prove it soon enough.

This would be my last day working at Albertsons. I walked home, scared and lost.

Hurting

I told a new friend named Jennifer (a straight-A student who went on to earn two Masters degrees and invent successful children's accessories) what had happened with the gun and what was about to happen with the guys out to kill me.

She told me, "Get out of there. Move across town and start over!"

On my way home, I saw a few guys with baseball bats in front of my apartment. They would hit the door and run. They were leaving notes daily now and threatening me every chance they had.

It didn't take long with this harassment to push my roommates to ask me to leave. I could not blame them. I was causing stress and anxiety.

Ivy came to my apartment with her friend and told me she had lost her virginity to one of the guys who was leaving these threatening notes. I was crushed and hurt.

She rubbed it in, so I decided to get with her best friend.

After that, she made sure to let them know everything about me. Talk about spite. I felt I was getting her back. She felt she was getting me back.

In the end, we were both out to hurt one another. I blamed her but needed to own blame as well.

Ivy had made sure I had to leave now, so I packed up and found an apartment across the street from the University of Nevada (UNLV).

ROUGH LIFE AND MORE FIGHTS

Trying to Make It Work

I was alone again, but had saved up enough money for a small 1-bedroom and invited Tim (the goofy kid I had protected) to move in with me. He joined me, and we went on job hunts. I found a job at Subway right in front of UNLV and my apartment.

I still had about $600 saved up and bought used furniture from a second-hand store. This store bought old casino furniture and sold it cheap.

After about a week of working, I walked through my front door to nothing. Tim robbed me of everything I owned. He took all of my money, every piece of my furniture, and all of my clothes. He did not leave me so much as a change of underwear.

Most of the problems I faced during this time was from protecting Tim. So I felt I was helping this kid out, only to lose it all. I wanted to hurt him. I wanted nothing more than to beat him like there was no tomorrow for him. I searched and searched for him whenever I was off of work and would hang out in front of the 7-Eleven to try to catch him.

Aaron and Leyland

This was when I met a guy I went to high school with named Aaron. I befriended him and his sidekick Leyland.

Both Aaron and Leyland were homeless, so I opened the doors to them. I would bring home sub sandwiches, and they would beg for spare change to buy food as well. I got Aaron a job at Subway, and we had a good thing going.

So much happened during the time at this store. One day the police ran a sting operation and handcuffed two perpetrators.

Another time a 7-foot tall white supremacist started a fight with a huge guy over 300 pounds because he called his girlfriend an "n lover."

They threw each other all over the store. Blood splashed on the front of the glass, and I ran to call the police.

The girlfriend ran back and said, "If you call the police, we will end your life."

Aaron also made enemies with the same guys that I had, and that is why he had moved across town too. Aaron had long hair and was a guitar player. Leyland was definitely his sidekick. He was always kissing up to him, and I believe he idolized him or crushed on him as well.

Together we would try to pick up college girls and had a lot of luck at it. We would always bring them home to our little ghetto apartment.

Aaron and I both had income coming in, and Leyland became more of a mascot than one of us. He would not work. Instead, he believed he would 'spare change' enough money to eat and live with us for free. We were mean to this poor guy. We had him sleep on a kid's bed in the closet. We thought if he did not want to work, that was all that he deserved.

Our boss at Subway took good care of us. I was left on lunch shifts solo so he could make his bonus. He would repay us with alcohol. He would get us two-liter bottles of Purple

Passion with Everclear, and we would get drunk every single night. Either that or we would drink 40-ounce sized Old English.

All we did was drink, work, party, and repeat.

One day we went to Aaron's old neighborhood and were spotted by that whole crew of Drifters. We ran as fast as we possibly could. A few of our friends got caught and beaten up pretty badly, but we got away.

This made Aaron and me realize it was not safe on that side of town anymore. We felt as if we were being hunted. We were basically exiled to our piece of town. We had worn out our welcome over there.

On the bright side, I had done so well at Subway that I was promoted to Manager. Just an 18-year-old kid and now I was managing my own Subway.

The owners of all of the Subways in Las Vegas had made a deal with the founder back in 1983 to open 50 stores within 10 years, and they were able to accomplish this amazing feat. They were desperate for new store owners and started a training program for us managers. I was chosen to be one of the first managers to go through the program.

I enjoyed working at Subway, and we all had the greatest of times.

Eventually, however, Aaron and I had to throw lazy Leyland out on his butt.

Aaron and I would listen to music, and we would work. We would always find girls to date. One time, we were both dating two sets of twin sisters. This was all routine.

Aaron let me know later in life that when money would come up missing in our drawer, it was because he stole it. He would use a hanger with gum on the end of it and drop it into the safe. He would then pull our deposits out and steal $20 to $40 at a time. The manager at his store let him go shortly after. I believe they knew it was him.

So now, I was the only one working. That was my time to leave and let Aaron fend for himself.

Brian

I moved in with two other friends and met a great guy named Brian. We called him Stumpy because a cheerleader from the college saw him passed out on the floor one night with his arm folded inside his shirt.

She said, "I didn't know your roommate was a stumpy."

I asked her what she meant, and she said she thought he was an amputee. The nickname stuck.

Stumpy came from an upper-middle-class family, and his roommate's name was Todd. They both worked at Little Caesars, where Todd was Brian's manager.

We added another roommate and decided to get two apartments across from one another. It was an awesome setup.

Brian and I were in one apartment, and Todd and Alan were in the other. They all had vehicles, so we could travel around freely. I had the sandwiches, and they brought all the pizza we could eat.

More Fights

It was a great time during those days, but the fighting didn't stop.

One day we were all on the Las Vegas Strip, and two guys in a truck cut us off. Alan started yelling at them, and they got out of their vehicle threateningly.

We were in a convertible, so I jumped out too and went up to the driver first. I beat him back into where his door was. His friend had a chain he swung around trying to hit me, so I beat him up too.

They took off and left the truck running on Las Vegas Boulevard.

One of the many times I fought on the Strip.

Life was all fighting and girls. We had parties five days a week and girls were in abundance. I worked out all the time and took pride in the physique I was building.

Todd decided to steal all of the money from the Little Caesars he managed and ran off to another state. Alan moved on, and Brian lost his job.

Again, I had nowhere to live.

Brian and I would stay in his father's old abandoned house and leave before people could look at it since it was on the market. Brian ended up moving back home, and I moved back to my old stomping grounds that I left two years before.

Back Across Town

With the money that I had, I got an apartment with four other guys — a junior 1-bedroom. We had to come up with about $100 a month each to make the rent. Two of the guys were underage, but their parents no longer wanted them at home, so they paid me their part of the rent payment.

Then, I met a pretty girl named Kristy, and we dated for three months. One day she and I were walking down the street with her best friend Alisha and my roommate Bubba.

A carload of Hispanic guys yelled, "F*ck her! I did!"

I flipped them off, and they screeched their tires and came after me. I told Bubba, Alisha, and Kristy to run.

When the biggest guy got out, I charged at him. I hit his head on his car three times and got him in a headlock. He bit down, and it sent a sharp pain up my arm.

The pain seemed so familiar. It was like what I experienced in the boys home.

I bit down into his shoulder, took a chunk out, and spit it out on the floor.

He screamed, "Get the gun! Get the gun!"

So I ran.

I ran as fast as I could. They threw a crowbar that hit my ankle. When I turned around, I saw the gun, so I kept running. I ran through the apartment complex, not sure if I would make it out safely. I was scared I was about to get shot.

I believe I narrowly escaped with my life. I still have no idea how I got away from that carload of anger. This was just another episode in the wild life I was living.

Another battle, but this one left a scar, a scar on my arm.

And this turned out to be the beginning of the end of another relationship. Kristy and I had never made love until she showed up on a Friday saying she told her parents she was going camping with her girlfriends.

I was so jazzed and nervous.

She did not believe in masturbation, so I had promised her I would not masturbate, and I didn't. So, I had about three months worth of build up and lasted all of two minutes. I felt like a total loser.

Sometimes things happen for a reason. Sometimes they are beyond our control.

After this, she refused to talk to me. She refused to acknowledge me in my own apartment. Five guys living in a mini 1-bedroom apartment and I was getting ridiculed, teased, and berated in front of every single one of them.

What a horrible weekend it ended up being. I was embarrassed and ashamed. I was humiliated and lonely.

My best friend at the time was a girl named Cathy. She had been with one guy in her whole life and ended up pregnant at 15 years old.

Her baby's father ran away to another state when he found out. He called her hurtful names, claimed he wasn't the father, and never looked back.

People can be cruel. He took Cathy's innocence and left her to fend for herself. I always wish her a Happy Father's Day as well as Mother's Day because she deserves it!

Homeless, Again

Around this time I ended up living back on the streets.

I knew of all the cubby holes, comfortable park benches, and where I could lay my head in peace. I was running around the same neighborhood, using the same park benches, and going through the same familiar, yet horrible routine I had done years before.

Then I ended up making friends with people in the apartment complex where I was laying around, and they hired me on as a groundskeeper. The girl who worked in the front office let me rent a room from her. I felt as if this was great job security.

I also met a girl who asked me to her high school homecoming and we dated for about three months. We had an excellent relationship. Her family had money, and she would show up in her Volvo so we could have our private time each day together. She would buy me food too, and I was never alone.

I thought this was something special, yet I found out that she was far from faithful.

For all the time I spent with her, she was spending quality time with someone else as well. I broke up with her right after Homecoming when I found out that she cheated on me.

It was dramatic. I poured a big gulp over her head in front of her friends and told her she needed a shower.

The next girl I met and started dating had fetishes that I was uncomfortable with. She asked me to hit her and choke her during intercourse.

I tried once to play along when she said her fantasy was to be raped, but I refused to hit her, and she got upset with me. She kept grabbing my arm telling me to ball up a fist.

My mind was blown, and I was sick to my stomach. I could not go any further, so I broke things off with her.

I started working out daily with a bodybuilder named Johnny whose claim to fame was he was high school sweethearts with Traci Lords (a famous actress). He got me in the best shape of my life.

One day I saw a kid picking on a little 13-year-old girl while I was cleaning the apartment grounds. I told him to stop, and he said that I would regret interfering and pay for it.

The next thing I knew I had eight guys pounding on the front door. They were all in the Blood gang. I knew I could no longer work on this property, so I quit.

I had been happy, building a life, and I was off the streets, but for how long?

While watching the news, I saw the last girl I dated — the girl with fantasies of rape and abuse — had been hit in the head with a rock. She was raped and found dead in the desert.

FROM THE DEPTHS

I was in disbelief. She always wanted to be raped and that was the last thing that happened to her as she took her final breath.

I was crushed, jobless, and now homeless again.

Also during this time, I saw that an ex-roommate had been up at Lone Mountain and was forced to lay down on the ground. Someone put a shotgun to the back of his head and pulled the trigger. He was executed because his father was in the police force.

So much violence.

Back in the apartments, I saw two of the guys who were going to jump me earlier. They were at my front door. I was with a friend who held my jacket as I approached them, ready to fight.

The tall guy was getting the best of me while we were throwing punches. He was about 6'3" with long arms. I figured he had a boxing background because he was beating me up pretty good. I was taking an ass whooping.

He broke my nose. I had blood flowing down my face and realized I could not win this fight standing up. So, I decided to take him to the ground.

That is when I started to turn the fight.

Once I started to get the better of him, his brother kicked me in the head twice. I was dazed. And he punched me one last time. I let out a loud scream, and they ran. I gave chase through the apartment complex, but they got away.

I was beaten up pretty badly. Both of my eyes were black, my nose was broken, and I had nowhere to go. I had nothing more than the clothes on my back.

My friend Mark, who also lived in the same apartment complex, asked his father if I could stay with them. Emilio was an older Cuban boxer who loved teaching us how to fight.

We had no money, so we got creative making food. He taught me how to make gourmet hot dogs. We would season a hot dog, wrap it in aluminum foil, and throw it in the oven.

Popping open a can of cold vegetables was our norm. So gourmet hot dogs was something special.

Mark had a speech impediment, and people teased him all of the time. He would be fine in normal conversation, but it started around girls and always got worse. I looked at him like a little brother.

Emilio let me stay with them for about a month, then I was back out on the streets again.

However, while his father was at work, Mark would let me back in to shower and hang out.

One day we went to visit Mark's friend Timmy, and I saw this beautiful woman who had just moved to Las Vegas. It was Timmy's cousin.

Her name was Katie.

KATIE + SACRAMENTO

Meeting Katie

Katie was close to six feet tall and had long brown hair with hazel eyes. She had an attitude to match her looks too. She was pretty fierce. We hit it off from day one. I would ride my bicycle to see her daily. We would flirt around, watch movies, or just talk for hours.

First Time with Acid

One day my friends and I did acid for the first time, and we went to Katie's homicide detective uncle's house to go see her. The acid started kicking in about the time we were leaving. I did not know what was going on. I had only ever smoked marijuana up until this time.

When we jumped in the back of my friend's truck, all of the street lights looked like dinosaur heads that would melt into candle wax. I could not believe what I was seeing. The psychedelics had taken over.

I kept repeating over and over again, "The dinosaur heads are melting into candle wax."

And the two guys saw the same thing. "We see it, maaaan. We see it."

Weird as it may sound, this experience opened my mind. I felt like a different person. I saw trees breathe, the leaves turn into a kaleidoscope, and my feet sink a foot into the ground.

We ended up climbing the side of Lone Mountain. I started a little fire and watched the flames dance. I had a pack of matches and a bus route guide and turned it into something I deemed beautiful at that moment. The fire was both sensual and mysterious. I felt like a pyromaniac by the time the acid trip ended.

I have heard so many horror stories about acid, mushrooms, and other psychedelics and was lucky this was a great experience.

The next time, I would know what it was like "to have a bad trip."

Relationship with Katie Grows

Not too long after this, Katie moved across town. I would ride a bike over 10 miles to see her every single day. I applied for food stamps because I was barely eating. I had been going hungry on the streets.

Then one day, Katie told me that the people at the convenience store told her how I got her food. I was humiliated, and my pride left me. I believe that this was the beginning of my breaking free from the welfare system. We had been raised to believe that welfare was free money. We never knew any better growing up.

Katie's mother was very nice to me and would let me take naps at her condo when Katie's father was at work. She would make me a sandwich and treated me very well.

I believe this was the beginning of my transformation.

One day I went to my mother's apartment. She had moved back with her longtime boyfriend from California, James. But she was cheating on him with another guy named Jimmy Hendrix. I had nowhere to go, so I asked her if I could crash at her place. She told me to find a car or a dumpster or something and crash there. I punched her front door until my knuckles were bloody.

I had lost whatever little respect I had for her then. She was not doing drugs but was definitely still an alcoholic.

Most Embarrassing Moment

Not too long after, my best friend Brian got an apartment and asked me if I wanted to stay with him. Brian was a great guy, and we had been homeless together before. I was ecstatic to have a place to lay my head at night.

I got a job at Winchell's Donuts and was able to make my share of the rent. It was tough though. I had to get to work by 4 AM but did not have a car, and the bus system didn't run in the direction of the store. So, I had to walk for an hour each day just to get to work.

One day while walking to work about 3:30 AM, I had an upset stomach and could not hold it until I got to the store. In desperation, I grabbed someone's Sunday paper and squatted down next to a tree in a cut out of an apartment complex. Right when I started letting loose, a car of attractive women pulled up. I felt as if a volcano were erupting, right as they turned on the brights of their car.

They started honking the horn and shouting, "Whatcha doin' over there? Are you taking a shit?"

I was humiliated in my red work outfit. I could not believe they put their bright lights on me and continued to honk away. They were relentless and laughed hysterically. The people whose newspaper I stole to do my dirty deed woke up and were pretty upset that their Sunday paper was being used as toilet paper.

I cannot believe I just shared one of my most embarrassing moments with the whole world. But, hey, we all have them, right?

A Baby?

At this time, Brian and I lived two blocks from Katie's parents' condo. She and I were inseparable. Whenever I was not working, I was with her.

We were two broken kids trying to act as one whole person.

However, two broken people rarely work out. Two broken people can help each other fill the void for a while. But sooner or later, you need to grow into a whole person. If not, your days will surely be numbered.

One day, we had a party at our apartment, and when I carried Katie home, she started throwing up. Once inside her grandmother yelled up to her father, "Harold, Katie's pregnant!"

Harold was a lumbering ex-marine construction worker who was close to 300 pounds. He scared the living shit out of me. I heard him running up the stairs, and I thought I was a dead man. He yelled at us both, told us to be smart, and warned me that if she was pregnant, I better do right by her.

FROM THE DEPTHS

We took a test, and it came back positive.

I had a family; I was going to be a father. Katie moved in with Brian, his girlfriend Tiffany, her daughter Destiny, and me.

(Tiffany had taken me in earlier when I was homeless, and I would watch Destiny for her so she could visit Destiny's father in prison.)

We made our apartment a home. This would be the family I never had and always wanted. But the girls got caught stealing plants off of the porches of our neighbors, so we were evicted.

Brian and I had a falling out because I called Tiffany a name. He grabbed a hollow pole and broke it across my rib cage. He ran, and when I caught him, I pinned him under my knees.

I loved the guy too much to hurt him.

I wished him all the best, and Katie and I moved into our first apartment alone. She ended up with stomach pain and started bleeding, so when we went to the hospital, they said to take it easy. We did not know if we had lost the child.

Her father was furious. He yelled at us that we had made up the pregnancy and that we were no good pieces of shit.

Not long after, we found out that we did lose the baby. Katie's father yelled at us again. He claimed that we knew we were never pregnant and called us cruel names.

We were crushed that we lost our child. We were both longing to have a family of our own. So less than a month later, she was pregnant again.

Sacramento

Katie's parents moved to Sacramento, and we had gotten money from a car accident we were in, so we helped them move and stuck around. While living in California again, I went to work for an apartment complex that taught me how to be a painter.

At 20 years old now, I had acquired two trades under my belt.

Sacramento was a lovely town, but I found it to be very boring. I missed my friends, as did Katie. Her father was horrible too. He could not find a job, so he kept borrowing money from us.

So, we decided to move back to Las Vegas when Katie was close to five months pregnant.

BACK TO LAS VEGAS + BABY JOSHUA

Building a Life

When we moved back, I got a job painting for a large apartment complex, and we purchased our first vehicle.

I learned to work a spray rig and painted all of the apartments in an 840-unit complex. They gave us a significant discount on rent, and I got to see Katie during lunch or whenever I would go home.

It was a good life. We even had a dog named Gizmo. He was a small, black Peek-a-Pom who would do handstands whenever he would urinate. He was a rockstar, and all of the kids in the complex loved him. He was an awesome little puppy.

Not too soon after, our beautiful son was born.

Joshua

Joshua Eli was a name I thought up when I was younger. I grew up in the High Desert around Joshua trees, and his middle name was after my brother I had not seen in over 10 years.

He was the light in my eye. This wonderful child would help me achieve greatness. I needed to be better for him. I wanted to be the role model I never had. I wanted him always to know how much I loved and adored him.

I also wanted my little brother to know — whenever I found him — how much I thought about and loved him. He was always in my mind and my heart.

Katie went into labor while I was at work. I ran home, and we went right to the hospital. Giving birth took about 19 hours. She was miserable and in so much pain. We were kids ourselves, and I hated watching how much pain she was going through.

The doctor had to cut her open and use forceps to help get Josh's head out. I was the father of a handsome, little, red-cone-headed baby boy.

This little baby boy was all ours.

Drifting

After Joshua's arrival, Katie seemed distant and lost. She had preeclampsia (toxemia), so we were lucky she made it through the birth alive. By this time, we had lost ourselves. I worked every day while she stayed home and barked orders.

She was never happy. She used to be mean toward the world and not me. That changed. Now she was mean to everyone.

My days consisted of waking up and taking Gizmo out for a walk, working, coming home for lunch to watch Joshua, take Gizmo for another walk, and make my own lunch. Katie would eat what she had made for herself. Once I got home, I would take Gizmo for another walk and watch Joshua until we went to bed.

This was an everyday thing.

I wish I could have helped her more then. But we were falling further and further away from one another. Sometimes love fades, or you realize it was not love but just teenage lust.

Still, I would have done anything to make sure I was able to raise our son. We never heard of Postpartum Depression, and if we had, maybe things could have been different. Back then, everything did not have a diagnosis as it does now. And we were living with it every day and in every way.

I asked Katie to help, but in response, all I got was a letter on the front door saying that she was moving in with her parents. I was crushed.

She left me without so much as talking to me.

I ended up drinking and met this beautiful girl who kept telling me how I deserved better. I thought about it and agreed with her. She and I ended up getting a little hot and heavy, and she told me she was still a virgin. I froze and knew I could not do this to her or my son's mother. No woman deserved to lose her virginity to someone who was lost, drunk, and hurt.

I knew I was not a cheater and had never cheated before in my life.

I opened up to Katie about it and got an ultimatum: marry her or she would move out of state and find my son another daddy. This was my worst nightmare. I always longed for a father figure and now was being threatened with my desire to be one.

Katie and I had drifted apart so I didn't see marriage as the best option. However, now it was get married or lose my son for good.

Her parents had just moved back to Las Vegas, so everyone piled into our little 2-bedroom apartment. It was now Katie, Joshua, Gizmo, and me, along with Katie's mother and father (who were not working at the time) and their two dogs.

Luckily, her mother Linda kept the house clean and walked the dogs, so it took that stress off of my shoulders. Linda also helped with Joshua.

So, Katie had less and less to do.

I ended up getting a promotion to Capital Worker and took care of two apartment complexes. The second was across town, so I was not home as much during the day, and that caused more of a strain on our relationship.

Katie was so used to my doing everything that when she had to lift some of the load, it drained whatever goodwill she and I had for one another.

We still went through with it and got married though.

The Wedding

Two nights before our wedding, my friend Dane had a bachelor party for me. He had an apartment above a house that had a glass floor.

This apartment was like a novelty and had faucets shaped like penises and knobs like breasts. I still chuckle thinking back. You could also see his dog through the glass when it ran overhead.

Those days were unreal.

FROM THE DEPTHS

I had not been around my friends much since my son was born, so this was the best time ever. My friend Aaron was with me, and they had three kegs and a gravitational bong with a bean bag next to it. We drank and smoked until we passed out on a couch and bean bag, only waking up the next day.

My fiancé was furious. Katie was sure I had cheated on her. She slapped me when I got home right in front of my friend.

I explained to her I had not smoked in a long time and it kicked our asses. She let it go after giving me the cold shoulder for a few hours.

Then we went to a little hole in the wall place on Las Vegas Boulevard and tied the knot.

While walking down the aisle, she started her period. She had waited for her wedding day her whole life and figured this was a sign that it was cursed. Neither of us smiled the entire time. It felt forced and unnatural.

We had already drifted apart and were both marrying one another because we had a son together. The love and the newness of being in a relationship had worn off long before our marriage.

My nerves were unreal.

Our reception was at my grandparents' house. Both our families came, and it was lovely.

But we were just going through the motions and doing what we felt was right for our son.

MONKEY IN THE BACK

A New Career Path?

Not soon after our wedding, my friend Lee got a promotion at the company he was at for the last two years.

He had seen how hard I was trying, so he offered to get me an interview to work in his previous position.

Lee was the same friend who would pick me up when I was sitting on park benches a few years earlier, get me a sandwich, and hit on girls with me.

He worked in a small prosthetics and orthotics company making back braces. It was a mom and pop shop.

It was only entry-level work, but I found it very fascinating. Lee said it was a pretty easy job with a bunch of good people.

I told my mother and Katie about the offer, and they both said, "No."

The Interview

Since I had no education, they said that I would be stupid to leave a job where I had just gotten a promotion. I was making $16 an hour, and there was no way I could make that at the prosthetics company.

But I took the interview behind everyone's backs anyway, just because I wanted to see what it was all about. I yearned to do more, to be more, to learn more. I wanted to help others, and this could be my ticket to making a positive difference in people's lives and our ticket to a better life for our family.

I wanted to set an example for my son. I wanted to show him that we can accomplish our dreams no matter what obstacles are in our path. We can overcome.

I wanted to be the role model I never truly had.

Obstacles are put in front of us to give us strength.

I never complain about living a hard life. I am thankful for it and always will be. I also wanted good karma from helping the hurting, the lost, and the disabled.

This was the perfect opportunity for me. I had finally found my calling.

My interview was with a lady and two older men named Rudy and Walter.

Rudy was a larger-than-life Italian who looked like he belonged in some old Mafia film, cursing and shooting up the place. He swore so much you would have thought he invented cursing.

Walter had a Southern drawl and was a nice guy.

They all were very honest and said they weren't offering anything close to what I was making at my current job. It would be $7 an hour, and my title would be "the monkey in the back."

They said that a monkey could do the job: it was monkey-see, monkey-do.

No!...Okay, Fine.

When I got home, I spoke with Katie and her parents about the job opportunity. Everyone was totally against it.

I said I would be taking a $9 an hour pay cut and that she would need to get a job at the daycare where her mother worked. Katie was not happy. I went against her wishes, even if it was for the betterment of our family.

She called me every name in the book before reluctantly agreeing to my taking the job.

LOSING EVERYTHING

The Beginning of the End

Katie and I kept drifting further and further apart. One night she went out with her friends and did not come home until 3 AM. I asked her where she had been.

"I don't need to answer to you or any other man."

That was the beginning of the end of our short-lived marriage.

I packed up my clothes and moved into my niece's father Ringo's apartment. He did not have an extra room, so I slept on the floor.

When my son was over, he would sleep on the floor with me.

Katie already had her family living in our apartment, so she stayed there. Later, I found out that she had cheated on me with a big security guard. His family had money, and that is what she had always wanted.

She threw away our future for the man she would have my son call "Daddy," just like she had threatened many times before.

He and I would see each other coming and going from her apartment. She kept leading me on, making love to me and saying how she wanted to make our family work. Yet she continued seeing him too. She blamed me, my job, what I had done after she left me for what was going on. I was crushed.

She seemed to hate the world, and I would get the brunt of the abuse.

A Shameful Night

We decided to file for divorce, and on our way to submit the paperwork, she started telling me about sex she was having with different men. It was graphic and hurtful. I asked her to stop, but she got even more descriptive.

I said, "We are on our way to get a divorce. Is this necessary?"

She continued, and I grabbed her by the arm. She started laughing hysterically and told me to pull over so she could call her uncle. He was a homicide detective and had been with the police force for over 20 years.

I followed her and asked her to calm down and talk things out.

She pushed me. She pushed me again. After shoving me three times, I had had enough and spat on her. It was disrespectful, and I own it. I should have been the bigger person but was not that big back then.

I will forever live with the shame of this night.

She punched me in the face three times and, the next thing I knew, she was on the ground. I had hit her close-fisted. I had struck her as hard as I could.

And now I would pay the consequences.

I blacked out and do not remember the exact moment or the actions. All I knew was that I was ashamed. I was not even a man. I asked the first person I saw to call the police. Then I waited for what it seemed like an eternity. I felt like I was the most worthless piece of shit in the whole world.

Was it reflex?

Was it anger from the year of mental torture?

Or was it a combination?

Losing Everything

I was not the man I wanted to be, and I was in shambles. This would surely lead to losing my son, losing my job, losing my whole life.

This was the beginning of the end.

When the police arrived, they asked what had happened. After we both gave our statements, they wanted to take us both away. I wanted Katie to go home to our son, so I said, "Please just take me." So, the officers did.

This was the only time I ever went to jail in my entire life. It was so surreal. It was dimly lit in the holding cell, and people were all lined up next to the phone.

Racial slurs were thrown back and forth as I picked up the phone.

"White boy, get off the fucking phone! Wait until later, mother fucker!"

Officers pulled me out of the holding cell and walked me into a private room. In that room was a Native American man I knew well. He was someone I respected, a gentleman with white hair and a massive snarl on his face.

He asked me what happened and I explained myself with a face full of shame and a heart that had been broken into a thousand pieces. I said it all. I owned what I had done and cried non-stop.

The next thing that happened will be forever ingrained in my head.

The man said, "You have always treated her like a princess, and she treats you like a dog. Run and never look back."

I felt saddened, but I knew I needed to try to move on.

The rest of the night I sat playing chess with another guy in the holding cell. The officers let me out the next day on my own recognizance.

I then called my place of business to find out that Katie had gone in and got me terminated. I cannot say that I blamed them. I would have fired me too. I also could not blame her.

I deserved whatever punishment I received.

No one could have been as hard on me as I was on myself.

A SECOND CHANCE TO BE A BETTER MAN

The Talk with My Job

When I went into my company to receive my last check, I requested to have a sit down with the owner and manager of the office.

They told me Katie had arrived with a black eye.

They were disgusted with me and ashamed of me.

I had let them down, did not deserve another chance, and they pretty much wanted nothing to do with me ever again. They told me that this company had no place for such a despicable person.

I told them I agreed and was so ashamed of myself. I told them the story of what happened. Tears streamed down my eyes. I was and forever will be ashamed.

I will always be honest enough to admit my faults. I served my night in jail, and I continue to live with the mental scars.

I felt I deserved so much worse.

Walter looked at me and saw that I was being sincere and gave me another chance. If not for his compassion at that moment, my life would not have turned out the way it has!

One thing that we all need to know is everyone makes mistakes.

Some mistakes are life-changing, and others are heartbreaking.

Resolve to Be Better

I will never forgive myself for the pain I inflicted on my ex-wife both physically and mentally. That day helped me evolve into the man I am now. I wanted to turn this disgusting moment into something more.

Being raised around abuse my whole life would not be my excuse. I did not do it because of that. I did it because I was weak-minded.

> **IMPORTANT NOTE:**
> I was asked to remove this story by different people, but physical abuse is often brushed under the rug. Society turns a blind eye to it. I am here to let you know that I own my mistakes. I may have none greater than this.
>
> I am truly sorry and hope that others can own their mistakes too. We can all grow from them. For this moment of anger, I will always feel sorry to my son's mother.

I needed to become a stronger man, a better person.

Strength comes from being able to walk away from bad situations.

Strength comes from using every trial to better yourself.

I wanted to believe *and knew* that I was better than this. Even though I was weak, I would never allow myself to be weak again.

I now hold myself to higher standards. I know who I am and would never allow myself to get to that point ever again.

ON AGAIN, OFF AGAIN

Katie Leads Me On

My soon-to-be ex-wife Katie and I did not talk for about three months.

New Years was coming up soon, and I started dating a girl I had known for years. She was my best friend since I was 17 years old and her name was Kelli.

We had been through so much together. She even talked me out of suicide when I was homeless and she was always there for me.

The big problem was she was in a relationship with her first love. I felt horrible, but it felt right between us. We would jam out to Pearl Jam and hold each other all the time. We had never made love because she was with her fiancé.

So she and I planned on spending New Year's Eve together until Katie called me and said she wanted a final chance. She wanted to make our family whole again.

I had just walked in on my mother having sex with my niece's father (Melissa's first baby's daddy Ringo), so I knew I had to move out soon. It was traumatizing for me and devastating to my sister.

Every day I had been going to and from work and then sleeping on Ringo's floor. But now I had to worry about my mother having sex with him.

My nightmares from childhood were starting all over again.

There were four of us in this little 2-bedroom apartment. I still had my career and got my son every weekend that Katie would allow me to. I was trying to be the best father I could be. So for my son's first New Years, I spent it with his mother. We made love all night long. She told me how much she missed our family and me.

I felt I had made the right choice.

The next morning, Katie got out of bed. I looked over at her and said I was happy we were working things out.

She said, "You do not know what that was?"

I said, "It was beautiful."

She said, "No, that was goodbye."

Can you believe that? She could not handle someone else caring about me, so she sabotaged my chance and then said goodbye. I was crushed. She laughed it off and told me, "Get over it."

Off Again

I left there broken, again. I felt as though I let my son down. I wanted nothing more than to raise him every single day. But, that was stripped from me. I made many mistakes and am at fault too, but my biggest regret in this life was not being an even better father for Joshua.

Even though Katie said it was goodbye and started dating a man named Fred, I went to see her a few days later. On my way to her apartment, I was cut off on the freeway by a car. I swerved back in front of him, and he bumped my truck.

I hit a wall going 70 miles an hour.

I saw I had a gash on my nose when I woke up on top of a small wall. My truck was still running so I tried to throw it in reverse but just ended up grinding the gears. I was in pain and bloodied up. I waited for the police to arrive.

They said they had no proof of contact from another car, so I received a ticket. I let a little road rage cost me the only vehicle I had ever owned. I allowed my anger to get the best of me, and now I had no car, no wife, and was extremely lucky to have my job.

On Again

The whole first year Katie was with her boyfriend (soon to be husband), she and I would mess around. I told him, but it didn't matter. He was just happy that she even liked him.

He was a bouncer at a nightclub and one day he I had words, so he and all the other bouncers grabbed me and threw me out on my ass. I was embarrassed. My pride was gone.

Not too long after, Fred and Katie separated. So, Katie, Joshua, and I got an apartment together again. I wanted to have a family more than anything in this world.

This was our last chance at reconciliation.

We rented a small 2-bedroom apartment, so Joshua had a room to himself. Katie was not working but seemed to be giving her all into repairing our marriage. We were both going to see where this took us.

FAMILY DRAMA + MARRIAGE CRUMBLING

More Family Drama

During this time Melissa, her daughter, and husband Aaron also needed a place to stay, so they moved in with us. My stepfather's daughter and granddaughter needed to stay with us as well. It was a madhouse.

We had nothing, but we were trying to help everyone. It is hard trying to save people who are unwilling to save themselves.

I just knew I missed my stepfather Jack while he had been living on the streets the last 10 years. He was a trust fund baby who at one time had millions in his trust account. The other homeless people would wait until he got his check and it would be a week-long party with motel rooms included.

He had a girlfriend named Irene.

When I was 12, she flashed me, and that was the first time I had seen a real woman's private parts that were not my mother's or in an X-rated magazine. I decided I would try to find my stepfather.

Melissa and her daughter came to help me find where he was staying. (When my sister was living in California, Jack would give her money or help out however he could.)

It was time to get him off of the streets. We found him and Irene cuddled up behind the dumpsters in their cubby hole. They had been staying behind the barbershop where his checks were always sent.

We had a good talk, and they decided to move in with my mother and her boyfriend. Dad looked so old now. The toll of being on the streets and drinking so much had caught up with him. They were both filthy and smelt bad.

But he was still my dad. I still loved him, so I had them join us on the ride back to Las Vegas. We got ahold of his trust, and they would be paying the rent at my mother's condo. It would help them all out and put a roof over my stepfather's head.

I would be able to get to know him again, as I had not even seen him since I was a little kid. This gave me hope in putting to bed the demons of not having a relationship with him (plus, we were told our whole lives that we would be getting a huge inheritance as well).

Jack had gotten old and had so many physical problems including chronic obstructive pulmonary disease (COPD). He coughed all the time but still had the sparkle in his eye.

Irene did not want to leave the streets and fought the whole way. She loved the life of booze, parties, and all the neighborhood guys she would fool around with. She lasted about six months before she made her way back to the streets. Back to her home.

The Final Straw

During this time Katie had her own thoughts. Little did I know, but my wife had some really shady stuff going on behind my back.

Katie's best friend was a Hispanic girl named Angel. She was very pretty, had a daughter, and was dating an Indian gentleman who had a few pizza places around the Las Vegas Valley.

He was nice, but I knew she was cheating on him with her child's father. Angel would borrow his BMW and have sex in it with her baby's daddy all of the time.

At the same time, a friend I knew when I was younger named Rico asked for a sit down with me and the Indian gentleman. Girls used to say when they met either of us that we were one another's doppelgängers. Rico had gone to high school with Katie and wanted to let me know she had reached out to him and they were having an affair.

She would throw a towel over our balcony to let him know when no one was home so he could have sex with her on our bed. I was furious and crushed. I wanted to kick his ass as well as shake his hand. He had destroyed me, helped free me, and helped me open my eyes.

This was the last straw.

I told the Indian gentleman how Angel had been cheating on him too. The next day, I went with him to Angel's house.

When we walked in, he went right to her TV and picked it up and walked out of her apartment.

She said, "What's going on?"

He said, "You are a cheater, and I am done."

I went to Katie and ended it as well. The next day, I moved out of the apartment with all of the families in it and got my own place a block down the street in a little ghetto 4-plex.

BAD DECISION: ACID FOR THE SECOND TIME

Stronger This Time

The next time I went to see my son, Katie knew I had a couple of traffic warrants and blocked the door to get me to stay and talk with her. I asked her to please let me go, and she threatened to call the police.

I tried to get past her, and she punched me. Right in my left cheek. I said, "I have another cheek." And boom: she hit me again.

I walked away as a better man. I did not strike her back and kept my composure. She wanted it to escalate, but I would not allow it to this time.

I knew I did not want to make it work with her anymore. I realized that I was codependent, just like my mother. I needed to feel loved, or I did not feel complete. I wanted to save the world, but I did not even love myself.

How can you love anyone when you can barely live in your own skin?

I had no idea how bad my mind was. I had no idea that I was a lost soul, but I was beginning to realize it and take the proper steps to get ahead in life.

Huge Mistake

This was when I decided to do acid for the second time.

It was a huge mistake.

Although I had a great experience in the park with a few friends who had taken it a couple of hours before me, they started to come down when my trip was at its peak. So they took me to my old apartment where my family was living.

I ran to the couch and grabbed Joshua's bouncy ball. I saw Katie's shorts on the ground, so I thought they were both there. I asked Melissa for help, but she and her husband told me, "You did this to yourself, so deal with it."

So as I sat there with this bouncy ball in my hand, I glanced at the television and the movie *Desperado* was on. All of the killing in the film was turning my trip even more. I sat on the couch for four hours.

The second movie was *To Wong Fu* where all the famous actors dressed in drag. I did not know if it was real or if it was the acid. I just knew that I was freaking the heck out.

I mustered up enough courage to run to my room and jump into bed. The sheets were red satin, and as the covers went over my head, I began to fall. I fell through hell and could hear Satan laughing at me on my way down. I will never forget that moment for the rest of my life.

For however good experience my first time was, this was the polar opposite. I felt like I would never wake up and would need to hear Satan's laugh for eternity.

When I did wake up, I was scared. I knew my mortality and that one bad drug use could take me somewhere I never wanted to go to again. This was the last time I would ever take acid.

I felt lucky to be alive.

THE DIVORCE FINALIZED

Sancho

While living in the apartment across the street from my son, I met up with a girl I had cared about since high school.

We had gone to the Homecoming dance when I was 18 and she was 17. When she graduated, she wanted me to join the Air Force with her.

She was the smartest woman I had ever met. She was beautiful and caring. She had a one-year-old son, and her husband was in the military in Korea.

I really cared about her and her family. They treated me well when I was homeless, and she was the same girl I bumped into when I was confronted about the gun by the police.

She and I had strange ways of reacquainting ourselves over the years.

I remember once I was trying to call a girl I was dating who had a phone number that ended in "1334," but I accidentally called "1333" and it was my friend's number.

We had always cared for each other. So when we reconnected, one thing led to another and we had an affair. I had never cheated on a woman, but I was part of this lovely woman cheating on her husband.

I was "a Sancho." I was the other man.

And I was despicable. This was something that destroyed me.

I respect the people in our military, so this to me was one of my worst acts. I am ashamed of myself, but I truly cared about this girl.

I loved her but wanted her to put her family back together. I let her know as much and, even heartbroken, I knew what I was doing was right. It was a moment of growth for me.

She and I, as well as her family, are friends to this very day.

I am glad to say that she and her husband are still married with two children. They have a fantastic marriage and are great people.

I wish them nothing but eternal happiness.

Angie

I then bumped into a girl that I had a crush on back in high school named Angie. She was married too, but he was abusive, did not work, and treated her very badly.

They were separated, and she had nowhere to go, so she moved in with me.

We had a great relationship, or so I had thought.

She spoiled me and made me feel loved. Josh was now three years old and was a lot of fun. He was always happy, and we got him a dog from the pound named Lucky Dog. Lucky was a little min pin with a big personality.

Angie drank a lot and so did I during those days. It was easy to get booze since she was a bartender.

FROM THE DEPTHS

She even asked me to come cross-country to Texas to meet her family.

Angie had physical problems, and doctors told her that if she did not to have a child soon, she never would. So, we made love in Texas, and I agreed not to use protection just one time.

That one time haunted me for the next nine months.

After we got back to Las Vegas, things changed quickly.

I knew I did not want another child but felt pressured.

Angie's sister moved in with us because their mom was heavy into meth and would dumpster dive right in front of our apartment.

It was humiliating when friends came over and saw her. But that was something I could relate to. Angie's mom made mine seem semi-normal.

We dated for close to six months until a friend of mine told me she was cheating on me with her husband in my car. They would line dance and then go full tilt in my ride.

How evil was this?

I understood it was her husband, but he treated her so badly and still did not work.

So, I told her that she needed to patch up her marriage.

She cried, but it was for the best. I thought that was the end of it, until a few months later I found out she was pregnant and she told me it could be either his or mine.

Mom

If you recall, my mother left the comfort of Maui a couple of years after I did and ended up back in the hustle and bustle of Vegas again.

Once my dad moved in with her and James, she went from drinking back to hardcore drugs. She started mainlining heroin again.

She looked like her old self when they would call her Skeletor back in California. She was going down the rabbit hole and this time taking my dad with her.

They got money sent to them from my dad's trust fund for different reasons.

For example, the trust paid for them to get a 4-bedroom home in which they could go about their scandalous ways. The trust also bought Melissa a car and gave my stepsister Diane a $10,000 check.

I did not want anything from anyone.

I wanted to be self-made and not to owe anyone or depend on a single person.

Divorce

Katie and I were still married through all of this.

She was back with Fred, and they had something to share with me. I was nervous but agreed to see her.

When I arrived she had tears flowing from her eyes down her face, and she cried out, "I am pregnant."

I was like, "Really? How far along are you?"

We had not made love in over three months, and she said, "Two months."

I asked, "Do you know whose baby it is?"

She said it was Fred's baby.

I wished them the best and told her that we were done and needed to finish the divorce.

We both hugged and cried.

Everything was amicable, and the divorce was finalized when she was about five months pregnant.

Jimmy Colson

TERRIBLE CAR ACCIDENT

Would This Be the End?

When my company sent me to take my orthotics exams, I decided to drive to Arizona.

Heading down the freeway in my Ford Explorer with a big front grill and KC lights, I saw a large truck in the distance. The road was only one lane in both directions. Suddenly, I noticed a big trailer trying to pass the truck. It was in my lane coming right at me.

There was clearly not enough time for the trailer to pass the truck safely.

So, I had three options:
1. Stay in my lane and get into a head-on collision
2. Pull off to my right
3. Cut off the large truck and pull off to the left

I had a mere couple of seconds to think. I looked over to my right and saw a 4-foot drop-off. I realized that if I went in that direction, my truck would roll over. So I figured it was better to go left and cut off the rig. I thought I would just blow an axle on my truck.

Boy, was I ever wrong!

As I cut off the rig in a near head-on collision, I felt air. I had jumped off a 25-foot concrete embankment. I felt as if I were flying. I passed out in mid-air, and my body went limp. It was as if I were in a bad dream that I wanted to wake from.

I do not remember anything after that.

My truck struck the ground, bounced, and rolled over twice. Joshua's car seat was flung 30 feet away from the car. I am so grateful he was not with me that day.

I woke up with my head partially in the windshield. Pieces of glass were lodged all over my body. I was covered in blood from a gash on my nose, and a big chunk of glass stuck out of my arm.

I am having surgery next month (in late 2018, as I write this) to take out the last remnants of glass from the top of my head that have been calcified over the last 20 years.

I leaned back and could not move at all. I was paralyzed.

A man ran up to the truck and told me that he had called the paramedics but was not sticking around. So, I was left in this ditch paralyzed, frightened, and utterly alone.

What would become of me?

Was my life ending or would this be another awakening?

Would this test be one that I could bear?

Would this be just another painful chapter?

Starting to See What the Future Could Be

I had a moment of clarity once my toes began to wiggle and I saw a glimmer of hope in surviving. I plotted out a future that I would lead if I got through this. I would become an orthotist and become the man that I wanted to be.

I would make a positive difference in this world, even if it were only one patient at a time. I was somebody and wanted to scream it from the mountaintops.

At that very moment, I did not know if I would be doing the screaming from a wheelchair or not. Would I ever walk again? But it didn't matter.

I started to be able to move my fingertips as even more dreams entered my head. I wanted to own my own prosthetics and orthotics company. This moment of clarity was an opportunity for growth. I would use this as a springboard to make a better life and be a better version of me.

I finally heard the paramedics in the distance. The nearest hospital was close to 40 minutes away.

The ambulance took me into the hospital, and the physicians evaluated me. They said that if I had not blacked out once my truck jumped, I would have broken my neck. I would have been paralyzed and possibly even dead. By passing out, I was limber and got out of this accident very sore but still alive.

Life is full of moments where one little thing could have transpired differently and your life would have changed completely. This was one of those times. This was one of those life-altering moments. I had lived through so much already, but this was different. This single instant could have cost me my life. At this moment, I knew I must find a better way. I must be a better me. I must live a better life.

While I was lying in bed at the hospital, I called my sister and her husband to come to Arizona and pick me up.

They said it was too far away. "You did this to yourself. You are on your own."

So I called my boss. He sent his daughter Julie out to Arizona to pick me up. She will always hold a place in my heart for doing this for me. I was lost and alone in a different state. I was battered and bruised, stitched and bloodied. But she came. She brought me back.

Afterward, I took my exams and did not miss a single day of work. The patients in the hospitals told me I had a bed next to them for me to sleep in if I needed it. I had rug burns on my head, stitches on my arm and nose, and pain shooting up my back and spine all the time.

Pain Killers Take Hold

This is when I started to abuse prescription drugs because they were giving me 120 Percocet 10s and 120 Xanax bars a month. I am one of the lucky ones who only took what I was prescribed, but it was still way too much.

I justified it in my mind that if they prescribed the medication, then it was all right for me to take.

Now I believe that our country has a problem with dispensing too much medication and not letting people know how addictive they truly are. So many people are using the medications, getting hooked, and starting down the path to far worse addictions.

The pills kept my mind altered and prevented me from facing realities during this time, for longer than I wish to admit. The reality was that I was in a lousy relationship and things needed to drastically change if I wanted to make something better of myself.

CRAZY TIMES

Wild Man

Now it was a crazy time in my life.

I turned into a wild man. I had so many relationships, but I was always honest with the women. I never said, "I love you" if I did not mean it.

I never lead anyone on to thinking a relationship was anything more than it was.

If I really liked someone, I would not date any other women. But, I would go a couple of years before my next serious relationship.

One day, my stepfather's daughter Diane came up to me and asked if I wanted a back massage and I said, "Sure."

She started huffing and puffing (in a sexual way) and cooed, "Just think if we were together when Dad passes away, we would get twice as much money as Melissa."

I was mortified and disgusted.

How dare this woman I was trying to treat as a sister come on to me?

I told her that would never happen and expressed how I felt. So, she asked Dad for money and moved back to Florida with her daughter.

Melissa and her husband Aaron moved across the street from me into a little ghetto complex of 4-plexes, and they went through a continuous roller coaster of either being deeply religious or high on drugs.

One day they were Jehovah's Witnesses, the next day they were next meth addicts.

Struggling to Be the Father I Wanted to Be

During this time it was harder and harder to be a great father.

I had my son every weekend, but Katie and his new stepfather Fred would bad-mouth me every chance they had.

I felt so sorry for what Joshua had to deal with but refused to say a negative thing about Katie. I thought he needed to have some stability, so I just took the blame for everything.

Joshua would soon have the first of his two little brothers too. But he felt alienated and alone. It was hard for him because he wondered why Mommy and Daddy were not together. I always told him we just were too different and we drifted apart.

Joshua was my whole heart, but he gave me so much attitude.

You could tell he was depressed; he started gaining weight and would not open up to me. He had a problem with depression, and I had no way of being able to help him come out of his shell. I wish I could have taken all of the stresses and fears off his shoulders.

I wish he had opened up to me more.

I wish, I wish, I wish.

I wish I could take all of his pain and make it my own. However, some wishes are impossible to grant.

I wish I knew how to be a better father. I look back and believe I did the best I could for being so young and not having any positive male role models of my own.

But I wish I had been better. I wish that the distance between Josh and me would have been smaller and that I could have bridged whatever was keeping us apart.

I wish his mother did not hate me so much. I was always a bad topic of conversation.

25 Years Old

I met a girl, Ashley, during this time who had a one-year-old princess named Leanne.

Ashley was 18, and I was 25. She was pretty, had a lot of energy, and had a nice smile with a little gap between her front teeth.

Leanne's father was absent. Ashley and I dated for about three months before we moved in together in a little 2-bedroom apartment attached to the company I worked for right in the heart of the ghetto.

She had a job too, and we were starting to get ahead.

Her mother was a lot like mine and was a big-time drug addict well-known around Las Vegas as Scary Sharri. She was a meth maker too with meth labs all over town, in cars, and in other cities. She ran a big crew of addicts. They were ruthless.

But Ashley hated drugs and I felt the similarities in our mothers made us kindred souls.

Our relationship started off great, but then it all changed. She started taking the medications I got from after the car accident.

That lead into her joining up with her mother behind my back. She was doing meth now too.

Ashley was slamming it with my mother and Melissa. They would tie each other off and get into drugged out parties while I was at work.

This all went on for three years.

Leanne's father even tried to start a fight with me. He was a professional heavyweight boxer and I saw him walking down the steps, taking an angle to launch at me. I told him to wait a second.

"You are a professional boxer, and I make prosthetic arms and legs for a living."

I acknowledged he would beat me to a pulp. But, I told him when I was done, he would remember me.

I told him I would bite his nose off and poke his eyes out. I told him that he would probably kill me, but he would always remember my face. He would be haunted by me and what I would do to him.

So, he walked around me and left.

Ashley always got me into fights. One time she told me a guy in a Raiders jacket threw a beer bottle at her and her daughter. She said he called her a dumb white bitch, so I found him at a bus stop, and we fought.

He got me in a headlock, but once I hit him in the kidneys he let go, and I broke his nose. I heard a loud snap. He had pulled out a knife with a huge blade.

I ran to the other side of my car.

He chased me in circles screaming, "I am gonna shank you!" He then cried and said, "Look what you did to me!"

He said he was going to call the police. He opened the door to my vehicle with the blade in his hand and threatened to cut up my brand new car.

I said to him, "Hold up — then you will go to jail." I told him to call the police, and I would wait for them to arrive. He agreed. But when he went into the store to use the phone, I took off.

The drugs Ashley was doing got so bad.

One day I came home with the landlord. Because Ashley was passed out, Leanne had painted our television and her toy box in feces.

(The kid was a fecalpheliac. She would poop in the bath sometimes and smash it onto the walls. She always had a fascination with feces.)

I walked in minutes before our landlord to see the nightmare scenario. I had to throw a sheet over the television and a towel over the toy box. I sprayed as much as I could to mask the smell of feces and birthday cake that she had also gotten into and spread across two rooms.

It was a disaster zone, and I was mortified.

We were lucky that somehow the landlord did not notice. Or if he did, he didn't care.

The one good thing I got out of that relationship was that Ashley helped me find a detective who found my little brother once he turned 18 years old.

Eli Returns

Eli had been adopted out as a child by a loving Mormon family who fostered him. His birth father Jim had died long before of a drug overdose with a needle sticking out of his arm.

My brother was living in Utah and he decided to come down to see me. That was one of the happiest days of my life. I had missed him more than words can explain. I had dreamed of this day for ages, and now here he was!

He was always in the back of my mind and still in my heart. I never got to see him grow up, but now I could be his big brother again. My sister and I were such opposites, but maybe this would be different.

It was so great seeing him. I introduced him to our family, and we drove from Las Vegas to California and then back to Utah.

What an awesome whirlwind of emotions. I got to see family I had not seen since 1984. And not long after this trip, Eli moved to Las Vegas with his girlfriend Missy from California.

He and I had a lot in common. He was also a hustler. He would be my best friend. He was my family.

We were all coming together: Melissa, her family, Eli, his girlfriend, the rest of my family, and me. This was a great time in my life.

Back to Ashley

Little did I know, but the girl who helped me find my long lost brother was also cheating on me. I had no idea about that or about all the drugs going on behind my back.

I had only smoked marijuana and did acid on those two occasions. But she decided it would be funny to drop crystal meth into my cup of coffee.

I went from being angry with her to writing her poetry.

I was on cloud nine until I found out what she had done to me.

I knew Ashley needed help and we decided to put her into rehab. She went in a pill popper and came out an even bigger addict.

Ashley informed me that the therapists believed we needed to have our own apartments, so I got her one.

Part 6

The Spark of Change

REALIZING THE CODEPENDENT ADDICTION

A Kicked Dog

Although I wanted to change my life around, I was still in a relationship where Ashley would tell me I was old, I was ugly, I was dumb, she hated me, and she wished she had never met me.

She said I did not deserve her.

I started to believe all of these things.

I had lost all confidence in myself. I felt old, fat, unworthy, unloved, and unwanted. Still, a lost soul, aching to be loved and have a happy family of my own.

This would not be it.

When people use harsh words like this toward you, it is time to move on and as far away from them as you can. Your life is too precious to waste on people who put you down and do not believe in you or your dreams.

Anyone who tries to take your hope or belittle your goals does not belong in your life.

You are better.

I justified staying during all this because I was raising Joshua and her daughter Leanne as brother and sister. Leanne was a cute little girl with big green eyes and an infectious smile. She was also a holy terror.

Despite all of the verbal abuse from her mom, I loved Leanne as if she were my own daughter. I remember so much throughout my life. But I can honestly say that the years I spent with Ashley are a blur. I was miserable and self-medicated to the point that I only remember bits and pieces.

I was a man without a heart. I was like a kicked dog.

The world kept telling me that I was nothing; therefore, I became nothing in my own mind and heart.

When Ashley let a junky kid named Mark, who she had met in drug rehab, move into the apartment I was paying for, that was the final straw. This was the same Mark with a stutter who had taken me in when I was down and out in the past.

I was buying all of Ashley's food too, just so that Leanne had a roof over her head and food in her stomach.

Mark and Ashley were doing crystal meth together, while I paid for everything.

Goodbye, Ashley

I realized the only time that she would call me was for money, for food, or to insult me with mean names. I had enough, and I was done. I realized I could no longer raise her little girl and cut all ties.

That was one of the hardest decisions of my life.

I felt like I abandoned and betrayed Leanne. But I had to for my own mental health and sanity.

It was hardest on the two kids because they were raised like brother and sister for over three years. I had Joshua every weekend, even though court orders were every other weekend.

I also got him one month each year. I introduced him to good foods like lobster and sushi.

I taught him good manners and all I knew about culture.

I wanted him to have everything in life. I wanted him to have everything that I did not get a chance to have. I wanted him to know that he was and is always loved and wanted. He will forever be my first child and my only son.

Codependency

Without anyone knowing, I also started therapy during this time. I needed to find myself and wanted to be a better version of me. I knew I was above the names, the anger, and the hate I received from Ashley.

I just did not realize I was a codependent.

Codependency is just like all other addictions. Yet this addiction is to having someone by your side and not wanting to be alone.

I guess I inherited this trait from my mother. I do not believe she ever spent six months her whole life without someone next to her. It did not matter if he was abusive, physically or mentally. It was all par for the course.

My biological father was the opposite. Heck, he loved being alone. He could shut off the whole world years at a time. He could zone out into his own world and travel anywhere. One moment he was on Earth, the next on Mars.

He just did not want to live in reality. I guess the pills gave me a different realm of reality, as life was passing me by.

I could have rested within this and, admittedly, did for a few years. I am sure it took years off of my life.

How sad is that?

To take pills to mask your pain from reality only to lose years later in life due to the effects of the medication. I have seen so many take this path and never return.

I have seen so many friends die from drug abuse.

I have seen friends, family members, and patients alike all give in to this evil game of cat and mouse. All trying to escape reality when, if they could do a 180, they would realize life is not meant to be escaped.

Life is meant to be lived.

I knew I wanted to live and needed to escape Ashley and her cold, dark grasp.

When that day finally came, I was hurt, lost, and alone. But the best part was I was free. I was free of the names. I was free of the anger, drugs, and lies.

I was free to forge a new path, and that is just what I did.

SELF-DISCOVERY + MORE FAMILY DRAMA

Self-Discovery

At this point in my life, I was still discovering myself. I was a blank canvas that wanted to grow. I had anger issues and a very short fuse. I fought my whole life and never backed down from any confrontation.

I was immature, self-centered, and destructive.

I had something to prove to the world and had a huge chip on my shoulder. I felt I was invincible.

Monkey See and Do More

At work, I was seeing patients even though I was still only a technician. I was hired on to make back braces when people had a fusion in their spine, but the leaders in my company believed I was articulate, so they trusted me to see the patients too.

I was later told that if it were not for the people above me being lazy, I would not have had such a crash course in patient care.

The "Monkey in the Back" got his first chance.

I also answered the telephones, learned how to get benefits and eligibility, and deciphered insurance contracting.

They teased me relentlessly, "Hey, look! The monkey wears a skirt!"

But what they didn't know was that I was using this experience to grow, to further myself, and to understand every aspect of my industry. I was in full learning mode.

Rudy, the owner of our company, wanted to leave the company to his daughter Julie, but she did not see her future in Las Vegas.

So, he put the company on the market, and one of the largest companies in the United States purchased us to get a presence on the West Coast.

Other Side Hustles

I also worked another job cleaning the offices for my co-worker's cleaning company called Dirt Busters.

I was now making $12 an hour at my regular job and then working three hours a night for an additional $25 at Dirt Busters to make ends meet.

I used a $2,000 bonus to finance a friend who was selling marijuana. To pay me back, he would give me marijuana plus $100 every week.

I smoked quite a bit during this time, so it worked out well for me.

My friend had this going for a while, but then blew all the money working on his car and asked me for another loan. Then, he ended up handing the business over to our other friend who kept it going for six months, and when he blew the money too, they asked me if I wanted to take it over.

I decided I could use the money to better myself, so I took it on. I only sold to older, upper-class clientele like lawyers, older construction workers, doctors, and such.

These were good ole boys who just wanted to smoke and not deal with shady drug dealer types. They wanted to relax and not have to worry. They were the people who would help me begin to finance my empire.

During my days selling marijuana, I met many interesting people.

I smoked with doctors out of apples, soda cans, or little metal self-made pipes. Can you believe that? They would core an apple so we could smoke out of it.

Construction workers always made fun things like gas masks you could smoke out of or big 4-foot bongs.

Lawyers were a little more high strung and almost always smoked joints.

Special Time with Jack: My Dad

My stepfather, who was living with my mother and James because his trust would pay rent and utilities every month, was off the streets, but to walk in the house, you wouldn't know it.

It was bad. When visiting, you would have to step over filth and syringes. The smell was disgusting.

I felt for him because hard drugs were in his face all the time. Little did I know, they were feeding him the drugs too. He got hooked again.

He had been an addict his whole life and needed to escape, so I decided it was time to pull him out of there.

Jack moved in with me and had fun selling marijuana to all of the people who would come over. He made friends with each and every one of them.

Medical professionals would come over, smoke a joint with him, and keep him company.

The next day it might be strippers who would dance around and flash him their breasts or asses.

He was in heaven.

He would always tell me far out stories about when he was younger or what awesome things happened to him that day.

Maybe it was wrong to let him sell. But at that point in my life, it was all about survival and working to get ahead.

I wanted to make a better life for my son and me.

My dad had a blast and got to talk about history and politics with so many different types of people. His personality was infectious, and people loved Dad.

We were close. He was old, scruffy, and did not like to bathe, but I sure loved him.

I miss him every day, and as I sit here and look at my desk in between patients, I have him with me. I have some of his ashes that I pick up and say a little prayer to.

Mom and James at It Again

My mother and her boyfriend James had gotten into the drugs much too bad again.

They would even steal from me.

Christmas was the last straw with her that year. My mom did a bunch of drugs and stole Josh's money out of his piggy bank. We caught her red-handed.

She also ate all the insides of a pecan pie and had no idea what day it was or where we were. She did not even realize it was Christmas.

She tortured us throughout our childhoods on Christmas. This time of the year is supposed to be about love and laughter. But Christmas to me was more about trying to live through the horrible situations mom put us in.

Hell if I would allow her to ruin my child's Christmas too.

We went over a year without speaking after this. I refused to talk to her until she was clean.

My mother lost her apartment soon after my dad moved in with me.

Eli and I went there and rummaged through the trash, piles of syringes, and bags of garbage. It was so disgusting.

My mother and her new crew lived like animals. No, animals would have moved out of that filthy pile of muck.

FROM THE DEPTHS

My brother and I were so disgusted and almost vomited several times. What was left of our childhood lay scattered on the floor of this horrible place.

Our baby pictures were covered in trash.

We found Eli's baby book under dirty syringes.

This hit us in the gut. Used syringes and garbage covered the last relics from our lost childhoods. I will never forget this. This moment is permanently imprinted in my mind.

I loved my mother.

I hated my monster.

I loved the thought of who she could be.

I hated the person she had become.

I felt like all of these drug addicts were like a subhuman; they were put here to drain the life out of those who cared about them the most. I had seen it since I was very young.

Dad, luckily, ended up living with me for years. He was also here to watch my son grow. He might not have been there for me as much as I needed when I was a kid, but he was there when Joshua was younger.

Jack was in my first BMW yelling how much he loved German engineering.

He was there when I met a person who helped change my life too.

TINA

Nice Complexity

One day I was at work and an 18-year-old girl named Tina came in for a clavicle brace because she had jumped off of a roof into a pool.

She broke her clavicle, but that did not break her spirit.

Her insurance would not cover the brace, so the company sent her on her away.

I felt horrible.

She and her friend were flirting with me, so I asked my manager if I could pay for the brace myself. He told me to have her come back, so I called her. She said that she had received one from a medical supply company but was flattered that I wanted to help.

She asked me on a friend-date to sushi, and I was nervous like I was a little kid again. When we met, she said that she had a boyfriend but wanted us to become friends, and I agreed.

One day a couple of weeks later, she was in California and asked me if I wanted to go to a huge party in Redondo on the strand. I grabbed my friend Jason and joined her and her girlfriends.

Jason and I got a room and invited them all to stay with us. They did and that is where she admitted that she did not have a boyfriend. It had been a test, and she was happy we came to visit.

The next thing I knew I was in a relationship with a very complex person. Tina taught me to love travel.

We would jump in the car at the drop of a hat and be in Mexico or California. On any given day we would not even pack but end up on a beach somewhere.

We would buy clothes as we went.

Tina always told me I was beautiful and to never sell myself short. She bought me nice clothes and said that I was going to conquer the world.

I believed her because she believed in me.

She helped build me up to where I knew I was more. I knew I would own my own company someday, and about a year into our relationship it happened.

My friend Lee, who got me into the first prosthetics and orthotics company, told me that the longest-tenured company in Las Vegas was offering me an interview for a possible partnership.

MY FIRST TASTE OF PROSTHETICS AND ORTHOTICS

Not Just a Monkey in the Back

When I first took the job in prosthetics and orthotics, I was just a number. I was hired on for monkey-see, monkey-do work.

However, I could envision a future and would not let anyone or anything hold me back. My son's mother Katie wanted me to stay in painting because it paid a lot better. She never believed in me.

She would always tell me that I was nothing. She would reinforce what the whole world would yell from the mountaintops.

Do not believe it when people say, "You will never amount to anything."

Although we are programmed to believe what others believe, you must break the cycle and realize that you *can* touch the stars. You can have the woman or man of your dreams. You can own your own business. You can own your own home.

Heck, why stop there? You can have whatever you want. The cost is believing in yourself, hard work, and perseverance.

My own mother wanted me to stay as a painter as well. She always built me up as a child. But once she lost that gleam in her eye, she forgot the kind words and affirmations and replaced them with, "Are you a fucking idiot? Your wife is going to leave you."

These people — my family — were also the ones who would hold me back. They did not believe in me. But I believed in the profession. I wanted to help the world and finally saw a way to do so.

Look Past the Present and Into the Future

I saw a future in prosthetics and orthotics. I saw the light at the end of this long, dark, cold tunnel.

I saw a way of making not just a living but also a life. I wanted to help the world and was finally given a chance. I would help patients have a better present and future.

In turn, my life would get better, and I would feel more fulfilled. I would be able to start earning good karma.

I wanted to cure the injured and make a change. Even if that change was one patient at a time. I had now found my way.

Money was not an issue, even if it should have been. We had very little when I started working there. We had an apartment, the clothes on our backs, and a beat-up old Chevy S10 pickup truck. Oh yeah, and a 100-gallon freshwater fish tank with Oscars and African Cichlids.

Heck, if not for a settlement check we got after a car accident, we would not have had anything at all. I figured that money would carry us since I was going to be making so much less at my new profession.

The early days in prosthetics and orthotics were tough in another way too because I worked with chemicals all day long. The plastic Kydex material we used lets off poisonous fumes that I did not realize would lead to possible physical problems later in life. We did not have any windows in the back or an exhaust fan.

We also were asked to do stuff that I think back on now and cannot believe. We were asked to reuse halo braces. They would get the screws cleaned (we needed to torque 8 pounds of pressure into the patient's skull) and then we would cut new sheepskin. Some of these braces were very discolored from repeated use.

I did not know any better then, but I would never do this to my patients or employees in my own company.

What was asked of us back then was truly sad.

We also were asked to make scoliosis braces for patients (another company had the patent) before we even knew what scoliosis was. We technicians were left in the heat with no ventilation and treated, as they said, like monkeys.

I Finally Believed

But my hunger for knowledge and belonging would carry me very far. It would carry me much further than I could have ever dreamed.

I believed in myself when no one else would.

I believed even when I was being called demeaning names both at work and at home.

I believed that I would someday make a difference.

I have carried those beliefs with me in all that I do in life. I do not know any other way to live except in the moment. If you live in the past, you fail to see what is materializing right in front of your very eyes. You fail to notice the beauty of life in the here and now.

I will always set lofty goals and hold myself to a higher standard than most do. I do not lie. I do not cheat. I do not steal. I did all of the lying and cheating when I needed to for survival, but those days are passed and so are my shady ways.

I can say I am ashamed for all the bad I did when I was younger, but what would that do?

I can also say I am a better man now because I learned from those hard lessons and grew exponentially.

Believe in Yourself Too

It doesn't matter if you are that punk kid like I was. If you can find yourself and believe, you can move mountains.

You can see the world.

You can actually live life the way it was meant to be lived.

This book will lead you through many trials, and that is what each experience is: a trial of sorts. You need to live and write your own story.

For some, it is a straight line to ascend to greatness. For the rest of us, it is one test after another to see if we are worthy of the spoils that life has to offer.

We are the future, as are our children and our children's children. So what we leave as our legacy will be remembered.

If you are an absentee parent, believe me, that is how you will always be remembered.

If you put yourself first, people will see right through you.

You must realize that in order to ascend to greatness, you need to bring others up with you. But you cannot choose who. They do the choosing of themselves by showing you their determination and will.

I have tried to save many friends and family, but if they do not work hard enough or are unwilling to take a chance, you cannot do it for them.

They need to find their own way. They must discover their own path and choose which direction they will go.

BEST FRIEND TONY

Job Change

I had just turned 28, and my life was on the right path. The monkey in the back had found his way. No more cleaning toilets, no more hustling…or so I thought.

I had the interview with an older gentleman who told me that they would pay me what I was making, but would bonus me on what business I brought to the table too. I did not notice but my office manager from the company I had been with for the last 10 years was there.

I accepted the position, and when I walked into work the next day, I was called into one of the offices to speak with my manager.

He said, "We saw you interviewing with the enemy and you are fired."

I asked him how could he fire me after 10 years of loyalty and, "What kind of severance package are you offering?"

He told me, "Nothing at all."

I picked up the phone and called their corporate office and shared a list of infractions they were committing. Some horrendous, some out of pure laziness.

Corporate said, "How does three months of severance pay sound to you?"

I agreed and never turned them in. I thanked my manager smugly for my three-month vacation before joining my next company.

Meeting Tony and "Painting the Town Red"

The patient I had seen earlier that morning was paraplegic who would often bring in her best friend when I worked.

The friend, Tony, was a younger guy, handsome, and always full of an unreal amount of energy. He was tall and looked like he could be a movie star.

When he walked into a room, you knew you were going to have a great time. Tony was a part of a younger crew who were considered Las Vegas Royalty.

He and I became best friends almost instantly.

His father was a big shot at a casino, and other members of his family were also very well known.

Up until this time, I had never really cared to go out to nightclubs, but Tony was the true definition of a Las Vegas VIP.

He would park his Ferrari wherever he wanted and people catered to his every whim.

We never stood in lines.

We drank for free everywhere we went.

And we were always flanked by gorgeous women.

(I was in an on again, off again relationship with my girlfriend but was always faithful no matter what presented itself.)

It was a lifestyle I got into big time. I was learning to enjoy life.

Although Tony was still going to school, he was also a professional athlete and a producer. He had harems of women who would hand him money. Blown away, I asked why they did that, and he said it was the perks of being him, as he added a wink.

(I later found out he ran prostitutes and would collect money, drugs, sex, or whatever they would get for him.)

He and I partied hard.

The partying would start around noon and end sometime when the sun was coming up. When he introduced me to famous people, it was always as "Doctor Colson."

We regularly drank with celebrities and famous debutantes, and we maybe did a little more sometimes too.

Cocaine, ecstasy, pills, and all kinds of drugs were rampant at these parties.

I saw famous people do lines and then they would hand you a rolled up hundred dollar bill. If you did not partake, you were thought to be a cop or a nark and were never welcomed back. You would be blackballed. So it was your choice: up your nose or out of the clique. I chose the former.

I chose to ride this wave wherever it would take me.

In the nightclub scene, the majority of people are on cocaine. Ecstasy had gained a lot of popularity as well. Some delved into crystal meth, but for me, meth was evil. It took your heart, body, mind, and soul.

I watched too many friends and family members succumb to its evil dance. It cost me relationships, friendships, and it has cost many people I knew their lives.

Trying to Get Back to Balance

Tony and I had many great times together, but I realized the nightlife was eating me alive. My girlfriend Tina and I were doing coke almost daily now, so we started to pull away from the scene. That was no way to live.

Tony went to work and opened a giant production studio where they produced everything from game shows to pornography.

I focused on my work and taking care of my son, but kept in touch with Tony, and we would go out from time to time or just hang out at my house.

I was even tempted to leave prosthetics and get into production and promoting because Tony offered me a position making six figures.

But I knew about the underbelly of that world too. I saw Tony running hookers, selling illegal substances, and doing more drugs than I thought humanly possible.

I tried to have a couple of interventions with him, but he kept claiming, "I'm good, Brother, I'm good."

Even with all the craziness, I would never miss one of my son's football games or practices. Joshua was my life, my everything. I tried to be the best father I could be, but it was not always easy.

One day during football practice, Tina and I decided to leave a little early to get tacos. My son would not speak to me for close to two months after this. I was hurt and tried my best to mask the pain.

Katie got him to turn on me for anything and everything. I had to live by a different set of rules.

His mother, stepfather, and grandparents took turns going to his practices, but I was not allowed to leave even one single practice early.

Anyhow, I had a lot of time on my hands, so when my buddy Tony called me and said to meet up with him at a casino because he was out with a rock group from the 80s and too messed up to drive, I said yes.

THE WORST NIGHT OF MY LIFE

Tony is Loaded

So Tina and I went to pick Tony up and take him home. He was loaded. He constantly slurred his words and closed his eyes. I asked what he was on and he said, "Nothing, I'm just drunk."

He had already been at a music awards show and partied with a bunch of his friends. When I had to track this down (you'll see why soon), it was unbelievable that he was even able to walk still.

After we smoked a couple of joints with the musicians, I drove his Ferrari and Tina drove my car back to my house.

That was when he opened up about his mother killing herself. This darkness was weighing heavily on him.

And his sister had also just thrown him out of her house, where he was staying while his home was being built.

He was all of 23 years old.

He had produced music videos for some of the most famous artists ever to live and here he was in my tiny house opening up to me about life, love, and how it was so hard to do what was right.

I felt for him and asked what drugs he was on. He drank energy drink after energy drink but still seemed to doze off.

I told him to sleep in the guest room, and Tina and I went back to my room.

The next day was a holiday, so I went to see my family and Tina went to spend the day with hers. I figured I would let Tony sleep off his buzz and we would talk later about it.

Later never came.

Broken

I got a call at about 8 PM from Tina saying Tony's car was still there and she was with her family.

(To this day, I believe they knew what had happened. I think they went up there, saw more than they lead on, and decided to let me be the fall guy.)

When I came home, I went up to check on him. While walking up the stairs, I felt a cold chill, the hair on my arms stood up, and my stomach dropped.

I opened the door, and the smell of death overwhelmed me.

My heart broke. My dreams of what Tony and I would build together evaporated.

The empire, the dream, was all but gone.

A young man always full of energy was now lying lifeless in front of me. A man so full of talent, with greatness in his future, turned into a corpse with veins bulging in his face. Rigor mortis had already set in.

He had defecated in his pants. He was as cold as ice and as hard as a rock.

I went downstairs with tears pouring down my face. I had lost my best friend. I had seen all of the conversations about how we were going to rule the town disappear before my eyes.

I could have written the next chapter in his book.

His house was being built, he was a professional athlete, he was a film producer, and he was the most well-connected guy I knew.

He would have had a family, and we would still be friends to this very day.

I was broken, and he was gone. He paid the ultimate price for drug use. It cost him his life.

You must realize that drugs seem glamorous, but they take hundreds of lives every day. No one believes it will happen to them. But it does. I have lost too many friends and family members this way.

I felt that I had failed as a friend.

Often, I think back on what I could have done differently that night. Maybe when I saw him so tired, I should have kept him up? Maybe I should have driven him to a hospital?

So many questions with no clear answer, and no chance for a redo. Just painful memories and a broken piece to my heart.

I picked up my phone and called the police and followed that up with a call to his father. Tony's father, grandfather, and brother showed up at my house full of anger and despair.

I could not blame them. I loved him too, and I was crushed.

Death Threats

Almost immediately, I got death threats. Everyone was under the false assumption that I had been Tony's doctor.

Little did I know, but those introductions at parties of "this is Doctor Colson" would almost cost me my life.

I still made it to his funeral, and our mutual friend read a poem I had written about him. After the service, a gang threw me up on the wall and told me I was a dead man.

I was shocked and scared.

I refused even to go home. I had to backtrack the events of that horrible night.

- His day started with a man who is still on TV to this day. They snorted an eight ball of cocaine.

- He then went to a tattoo parlor and picked up morphine suckers.

- Then he took pills on top of all of this.

- He went to the music awards show and did ecstasy.

- He finished the night drinking alcohol, doing more coke, and smoking marijuana.

His body was on a roller coaster of uppers and downers. He had nowhere to go and reached out to me. I took him in, as any friend would, but I had no idea just how many drugs were at play in his system.

Now, I was dealing with all the backlash.

Since I was in between jobs for three months, I hid out at Tina's house where I got calls describing the color of my couches, asking questions about where I was, and demanding to know when they would be able to talk with me.

I presented all of the information I had gathered to the gang.

I explained that I was just the unlucky schmuck who wanted to help a friend out. I gave them evidence that I was not a physician. And I offered to take a drug test to prove I had been clean of any hard drugs for many months.

All of my sleuth work ended up saving my life.

I even had a hit put out on me for a while. I still cringe to this day and am always looking over my shoulder.

After two weeks of hiding out, I went home. Both our dogs ran over to the room where Tony had passed away and barked for over 10 minutes nonstop.

When we went up too, I almost vomited from the smell. Tony had thrown up in the bathroom, and it was now moldy and disgusting.

This was what was left of him.

Nothing more than a young life lost, talent wasted, a death threat, a beautiful memory, unfulfilled dreams, and a toilet full of vomit.

Drugs suck.

Life Still Spinning

During my time off of work, I had decided to stop doing hard drugs. I had been clean of cocaine, had slowed down on my drinking, and I wanted to kick the pills too.

My focus was with my new position.

I was now a manager, a marketer, and I was going to be a partner in a company before I even turned 30 years old. My dreams in my field were coming to fruition, but with all that was going on, it caused a divide in my relationship with Tina.

The strain of Tony's passing added to our breaking up too.

The stress, my psyche, and the phone calls she shared with him the night he passed away never left my mind or my heart.

I had found out they were texting when I was asleep. Texts back and forth at 2 AM were more than I could stomach. It was definitely a big red flag smacking me in the face.

I would not be surprised if they were up late doing drugs and who knows what else with him while I slept. And I believe Tina and her mother likely found him dead before I ever did.

Not too long after this horrible day, my friend Henry told me that he was going to Amsterdam by himself and invited me along.

I decided to use this time to get over the breakup and kick the pills.

And I ended up also discovering a new love called travel.

The thought of going to foreign lands intrigued me. Discovering new cultures, meeting different people, and making new friends was fascinating.

From a low-income family, our idea of travel was going to the Valley to take back stolen merchandise for money so my mom could get her next fix.

While in Amsterdam, Henry and I had a fantastic time, but I cried a lot for Tony too.

Finding Myself

My life had been torn in so many different directions that my head was left spinning. I was the lucky one though. I still had my life to live. The time in Amsterdam was a wake-up call.

I found myself after being lost for years.

I would come back to the United States and try to stay completely clean. I was not going to be another young life lost. I was determined to conquer the world.

OPENED AN OFFICE BUT WANTED MORE

An Odd Visit

After I opened my new office with the company that offered me a partnership, a man walked in with a prescription from my former company.

He had seen my not-that-common last name and asked, "Did you know that the Colson's ran the prison system in California under the Nixon administration?"

That was news to me.

This mysterious man then asked, "So, you are him?"

I retorted, "Are you Undercover?"

He replied, "I cannot confirm or deny that. But I will be back here to debrief you soon."

And he walked out of my office.

To this day, I never got the debriefing, nor did I ever see him again.

This day will always confuse and confound me.

Who was he really?

Why did he come to my office?

Why did I need a debriefing?

I will forever want to know to answers to these questions.

Start Your Own

Coming to the end of one year with the new company, I still had not received all they had promised. They made me do the work of three people but paid me even less than the company I was with previously.

After making $4,000 less than the year prior, I was called into the majority owner's office and I asked him how this was possible since they had promised me the world.

He cut me a check to break it even and then said he wanted me to take out a $41,000 loan against my home as a down payment to purchase a 14% stake in his company.

These numbers did not seem to my advantage.

I had lunch with a friend who owned his own prosthetics and orthotics practice and shared with him a few things going on with the company.

I told him about the lead prosthetist who had died of a pill overdose.

I told him about the other prosthetist doing mushrooms and being on trips with his patients.

I told him about all the broken promises.

He said to me, "Start your own company, kid."

THE BEGINNING OF MY COMPANY

30 Years Old

I had just turned 30 and was going to risk it all. I had a meeting with the owners of the company, and they said, "If you do not accept our offer, you will be fired right here on the spot."

So, I thanked them for the opportunity but told them that I would have to decline the offer, accept being fired, and open up my own business. Most of them laughed at me.

During the six months I received unemployment payments, I started pulling their clients over to me. (Eventually, they would have to close the office that they had built for me. I knew once that happened, I would take over their entire book of business.)

But, I am getting ahead of myself in the story.

I started by getting my business license, my Medicare provider number, and then I found an investor who was willing to bet $30,000 on me to help finance my dream.

In exchange, I had to give up half of my company.

My Company is Born

The investor financed the business, and I put in my blood, sweat, and tears. She chose the name of the company: Precision Orthotics & Prosthetics.

I was not fond of the name because prosthetics and orthotics are not exactly something of "precision."

But I accepted the name, and came up with the moniker "P.O.P."

The price of half of the company was steep, but I believed in myself. My partner was married to a physician and made me numerous promises. Unfortunately, she did not fulfill a single one.

I, on the other hand, did whatever they asked. Even if it was outside the box.

For example, that Easter the Easter Bunny they hired for a party canceled on them, so I filled in as admirably as I could.

Breakdancing in front of all the children, the kids asked me why I wasn't very good. Apparently, the regular Bunny was great.

Bunny on the Pole

After their party, I jumped into my car and went straight to a strip club because I was dating a bartender who worked there.

She had no idea it was me in the bunny suit.

I was totally incognito.

I asked the other bartender for a Bloody Mary and drank it from a straw.

On the loudspeaker, the DJ said, "Next on stage is the Easter Bunny!"

I jumped up out of my seat and tried my best on the stripper pole. I hit my groin area on it and remember thinking, "Man, these girls are good." Then, "Damn that hurt."

The next thing I knew two Hispanic guys kept yelling, "Hey, baby, take it all off!"

I said, "Stop guys. I'm a dude."

They laughed, and when I got off of the stage, one pinched my butt. I peeled off my bunny mask and told him, "This is the worst day of your life. You are about to get your ass kicked by the Easter Bunny on Easter!"

I chased them out of the club and down the street.

My temper was still a work-in-progress.

WHITE SUPREMACISTS ON PCP

The White Supremacists

One night, I was heading into a club when I saw two white supremacists walking out with fire in their eyes.

They picked a fight with two African American men (even though they asked them to stop) and then started fighting a group of 10 Hispanic men across the street too.

The first guy was about 275 pounds and 6'4".

The second was about my size, 220 pounds and 6 feet tall.

They were beating everyone up.

Then, a girl on a bicycle asked them to leave her friends alone, and the big guy lifted her off her bike by her neck and smacked her. She had blood streaming down her face and screamed for help.

I ran across the street as if I were Superman.

I punched the big white supremacist as hard as I could, and he lifted a giant rock to hit me over the head. A security officer friend of mine ran to my rescue and hit him with his mag flashlight. The big guy did not flinch. He continued to come at me.

Suddenly, we heard screeching tires, and he jumped out of the way. It was the second guy coming at us in a truck.

I jumped as the truck struck my legs and flipped me over the hood.

When I came to, I saw the security guard and the big guy in a vicious dance. One was waving a rock, the other a flashlight.

I then looked over at the driver of the truck who just struck me and ran at him. He threw his truck in reverse and hit his friend. I watched the big man's leg snap in half.

I kept yelling, "You hit your friend! You hit your friend!"

But he just came back at me with the truck and ran his friend over again. I jumped behind a telephone pole, narrowly escaping, and got the license plate number.

He grabbed the big guy, and they took off.

Later, when the detectives and Victims of Violent Crimes took over, I found out that they were brothers, were on PCP, and had taken the truck on a test drive and never returned it.

They were also in a car accident, and that is how they explained the bigger brother's broken leg.

Realizing Important Things

I had so many crazy adventures and physical altercations — so many death-defying experiences. But this was one that put fear into me.

I could not stop from helping this lady.

However, if not for his brother hitting me with the truck, I was sure to die from the skull-crushing about to happen under that huge rock.

The blank stare and glazed over eyes, man, I know I have a guardian angel because I saw my fate.

I knew I was not going to live, but somehow I did.

We all have these moments in life that have to bring forth change. I knew my days in the strip clubs needed to come to an end. I needed to focus on the here and now.

I needed to put everything into my business and son.

BUSINESS GROWTH + PARTYING TOO HARD

Business Growth

With my company, it was as if my partner handed me the money and then turned her back.

She made promises of aiding me in acquiring insurance contracts and getting her friends to send me patients. But she'd send their patients to my competitors when she was upset over the smallest of things.

After six months, my former company closed the doors to its Henderson office. I haggled a deal with the complex and had the company pay for part of the rent to get out of their lease.

I had warned them, but they still saw me as a joke.

Now it was my time, and this was my place. This office was built for me, and I would show them what they were missing out on.

After adding the signage and equipment, I had a total of $11,000 left to work with.

I started what has become a multi-million-dollar prosthetics company for just $11,000. I do not know how it was even possible.

But it was!

I now pay over $50,000 for individual prosthetic parts for my patients.

Myspace

Not too long after the grand opening of my office, my niece came down and told me about an internet site called Myspace.

My friend Shane helped me with my profile. We made the background out of blue DNA strands to let people know I worked in the medical field. My song of choice was Behind Blue Eyes by Limp Bizkit.

Everyone started calling me Jimmy Blue Eyes. I liked the name, as well as all of the attention I was receiving.

The early days of the company were very tough though. I had to do whatever I could to keep the doors open. I sold marijuana and used that income to stay afloat. I got a second loan on my house and refinanced it as well.

I used part of the money to buy my first nice car, a BMW 540i with a V8 engine, and also some nice clothes. I believed that if I wanted to become successful, I also needed to look and feel successful.

I was working solo in the company at first and could not afford an office manager, so I turned to a friend. Her husband and I had worked at another company together, and they bought their marijuana from me, so I asked if she would help me out. Thankfully, she agreed.

Then one day, when I was messing around on Myspace, two of the top ten girls on the platform happened to be in Las Vegas and liked some of my pictures. They were paid to travel around the country and go to the nightclubs. Myspace had made them famous, and they liked me.

FROM THE DEPTHS

I was in disbelief.

They had millions of followers and chose me out of the crowd.

They asked if they could come to pick me up in a limo and take me to dinner with them and one of the most famous boxers ever. How could you turn that invitation down?

I agreed, and when we were in the limo, we did a semi-hot photoshoot. Hair pulling, kissing...the works.

I went from being this lonely, regular guy to having some of the most famous women in the country taking ME out. This was the beginning of how Myspace helped change my life. The day after the photos were posted, I had thousands of people (mostly girls) send me friend requests.

When I would post that I was going to a nightclub, I'd have 10 to 20 girls ask if they could join. I still shake my head at how this happened.

One day, I went to meet friends at Voodoo Lounge on top of the Rio Casino and had 25 girls join me.

That is when the head of the club turned to me and asked, "Are you interested in getting paid to party?"

I did not know that could be a job. You could meet girls, get free drinks, and get paid for just being you? Once I knew it was a real thing, I wondered why it was not everyone's first career choice.

But warning: the glitz and glamour do fade out much too fast. So does being a club promoter.

Partying Too Hard

I accepted the position and the next thing that happened changed the course of my life forever. I was constantly marketing and partying. The company's growth was painfully slow, and I was tempted many times to drop prosthetics and orthotics entirely and jump into the nightclub scene full time.

The physicians all around the area took notice of my after-hours activities and wanted in on what I was doing. They asked me to take them partying too.

The club was happy because I was bringing in glamorous models *and* high roller doctors.

The models were happy because I was introducing them to doctors and getting them free drinks all night.

I was happy because I was able to build great relationships with the physicians without spending a single cent.

In the medical profession, they have laws in place so that you cannot pay to take physicians out. This didn't apply to what I was doing because I did not ever have to pay to take the doctors out. I was actually paid to do it.

I met beautiful women all the time. And I looked as if I had it all figured out. It was a dream scenario. I still pinch myself thinking back to that time. How was it real? This triangle of beauty, power, and promise would forever change my life.

I had carloads of women stay at my house when they came to Las Vegas, and when they did not find anything to do or anyone big to hang out with, they would end up back with me. I would wake up with three girls in bed with me sometimes.

The drugs, the drinking, the partying, and the sex were all stuff that I still cannot believe I did or even lived through. I am glad that I got all of that out of my system, but am also ashamed of the person I was becoming.

I went from being a young man who wanted to spend his whole life with just one woman to being a Don Juan of sorts.

I was always honest. I never led a girl on, never promised anything that I would not do.

I may have lost my soul, but I always kept my morals.

I had a friend who moved into my place too with his children. He would stay on my couch, and we would go party. He was part of this roller coaster, and I am proud to say he is a multi-millionaire now as well. He got into producing and selling CBD products and was also known as the King of Nightclubs for a few years.

He and I would come home with women, drugs, and drinks.

Women would travel from all over the United States to be a part of this crazy ride.

During this time, my company finally began to grow.

The doctors made sure to send me work in order to be a part of the never-ending party.

The girls were always there and very appreciative.

The guys who tagged along were enamored with how we were 'getting paid to get laid,' as they put it.

It was a win-win.

SARA

Meeting Sara

One day, I was dancing with three girls on top of the Rio in my VIP section when a fellow promoter named Wayne walked in with a beautiful bombshell.

She was the most gorgeous woman I had ever seen.

My heart skipped a beat as they had walked up to our VIP section.

She had short, dark brown hair and the most beautiful smile.

My heart skipped a couple more beats, and I knew I wanted to get to know her.

I went up to her and asked her if she could drop it on the floor just as the song *How Low Can You Go?* was on.

We danced a few minutes, and I turned to my friend and asked who she was. Her name was Sara.

I then asked her on a date, but she declined. She said she did not date nightclub promoters. I understood why.

She was paid to be at parties. They paid the most attractive women to be ambiance models and, man, was she ever a good one.

I told her that I had a day job where I owned a medical practice and the nightclub stuff was just for fun. We started talking.

Sara came to my VIP section a couple of times with other guys, and I felt so jealous.

She knew I had a son and also said she did not date men with children.

Two strikes against me, but I had not struck out yet.

A First Date?

One night we were at an after-hours party, and I asked her out once again.

She said that her mother and little brother were coming to Las Vegas and he was a year older than my son, so we could take them to the Circus Circus casino for kids where they could have some fun.

We went and hit it off great. We even held hands.

My heart pounded, and I wanted to get to know this beautiful girl better. Sometimes the little things in life are all that stand out or are all that you can remember. I can freeze frame the moment our hands first touched and thought how badly I wanted to be with this gorgeous woman.

One touch of the hand and my visions of nightclubs slowly dissipated, and I knew. I knew that she was the one.

I remember holding her hand and cherished those moments eternally. I felt like a little kid again.

We would soon become inseparable.

She was nine years younger and had a beautiful face, light brown doe-eyes, a devastating smile, an infectious laugh, and curves for days.

She had me hooked.

I did not want to fall in love. I could not fall in love.

Screw it, I fell hard for Sara.

Life was exactly what I felt I wanted. But sometimes — heck, all of the time — love chooses us when we least expect it or want it.

We never have control over who we fall in love with or when it happens.

We were living an enchanted life on top of the world in Las Vegas on the 51st floor. We could go to any nightclub and never stand in line, drinks were always free, and we were treated like royalty.

After a couple of weeks, Sara and I became intimate. It was amazing, and I knew this is who I wanted to be with. I knew she was to be part of the future I wanted to build.

I wanted to give her the life I believed she deserved.

Her life was rough, just like mine. We were two broken people who felt that if we put all of our broken parts together we might become whole.

Sara had been abused and given up for adoption at an early age. Her mother took the side of her predator husband, and my future wife was broken.

FROM THE DEPTHS

She harbors so much pain to this very day.

I will not go further into her childhood since she is writing her own book on how she survived such strife and turmoil. How she overcame more obstacles than I could imagine.

I commend her and love her so much for the strong woman she has become. She, like me, hopes to help young girls to know they are not alone. And she hopes that by telling her story, she can save lives.

Sara always wanted a better relationship with her biological mother. So, when she arrived home after making love to me, she decided to tell her mother, and that was the beginning of all hell breaking loose.

Her mother called her a whore and asked how she could do that. She called me crying, and I believe that was the moment I truly fell utterly and completely in love with her.

I wanted to protect and love her more than life itself.

I wanted to do my best for her as well as for my son.

Her mother and little brother went back to Michigan, and one day we were lying in bed talking about Hawaii and how stunning it is there.

I shared that I had lived in Hawaii and we realized that we both had always dreamed of being married there.

The next thing you know, I popped the question and asked Sara to be my wife.

We had been dating for about a month and a half and decided to elope and run off to Maui.

A Small Wedding in Paradise

We did not let anyone know about our decision as we escaped to our little piece of paradise. We were two broken people trying to make a life with one another.

We both yearned for a family and chose one another.

We chose to have and to hold.

We chose to make this the first day of forever.

With our upbringings, neither of us knew how to do things 'right.' So the beginning was extremely tough. Dysfunction was something we both grew up with, and it would take us years to break this chain.

It would take years of therapy and self-reflection for each of us.

We both needed to learn how to accept each other's flaws to be able to love one another's strengths. We also needed to learn to take responsibility for who we are and what we do.

I was paid to party and be charismatic.

Sara was paid to be beautiful and witty.

This was a recipe for disaster, especially in a marriage.

This is the reason famous couples tend to split up. They are torn in different directions; everyone wants a piece of them.

Living the party life always is a roller coaster ride, and I was getting motion sickness.

In Hawaii, before our wedding, we met up with my family.

I did not even have enough money to pay for the nuptials, so I asked my friend Ashleigh to Western Union me $500 to help pay for everything.

We both said, "I do" (actually, "Hone Hone" which means to kiss in Hawaiian) and became husband and wife. Sara had only seen me larger than life. Now, this got real.

My money issues had become real as well. I was putting on the impression that I had it all figured out, but that could not have been further from the truth.

Should I give up my medical practice for the glamorous life the nightclubs presented me?

Or should I focus on my practice and put my all into it?

There was no easy answer because I needed every cent I earned to make it through these tough times. My company was still in its infancy stage, and we were lucky to make a few thousand dollars a month.

Times were tough.

I felt I needed to be tougher.

Dad's Health Deteriorates

My stepfather was still selling marijuana, as was I. His health was continuing to deteriorate. His emphysema had taken hold with no way of turning back the clock.

He continued to smoke and got to the point to where he could no longer go up the stairs, so he moved into the garage.

We put a huge swamp cooler in there and asked him if he wanted to be admitted into a home. He refused and asked to be left alone and to live the remainder of his life the way he chose.

You could hear his coughing ring out throughout the house.

Barely Making It

I almost never had any time to sleep during those days. I know this was tough on Joshua and my new wife.

I felt for them, yet could not come up with an adequate solution.

While Sara and I were dating, she thought I was narcoleptic. I would fall asleep in mid-conversation with her. I would fall asleep once we were done making love. It was embarrassing, but she loved me and believed in me.

I do not know if I completely believed in myself during that time in my life. The truth was I had been doing a lot of cocaine to stay awake. I was putting in 20 hour days, so when I was able to get a nap, my body had no choice but to do so.

Cocaine can take you over and crush your spirit. You get a false sense of security and power. It is evil. Once you escape its grasp, you can see life with your own two eyes.

It will take everything from you if you let it. I would not let it.

I do not regret anything I did during this time. I would not be in the position I am in today. These were sacrifices that I felt were well warranted. Without them, I might not have made it.

But with them, I almost lost my life.

And to be clear, drugs did not help me get to where I am. They kept me awake and also almost cost me my life many times.

More on that to come.

I Am Sorry, Joshua

While I was a nightclub promoter, I felt I was a good father still. But looking back, I left a lot on the table.

I could not be as attentive or understanding when fueled by cocaine or falling asleep the second I was coming down.

I could not be as empathetic as I should have been when I believed I was going to conquer the world. I spent so much of my son's childhood just trying to live in my own skin and was, therefore, not the man I should have been for him.

For this, Joshua, I am truly sorry.

This will forever haunt me, and I apologize to my son with all of my heart. I did the best that I thought I could. Times were trying, and I was living a double life: I saw patients during the day, and I partied with famous people at night.

Drugs fueled me, and I did not know any other way to connect the dots. But I should have been a better man for you. I should have held you closer, showed you more love, and not judged. I should have been your champion, your role model, but I am merely a man with faults.

I own the fact that I am not perfect. I am far from it. But I always strive to be better.

Every day, when I awake, I want to be a better version of myself. My growth game has become strong. But back then I was still in a mode of self-discovery and made whatever sacrifices I could for the betterment of our family. Or, to be honest, for a better life for me.

That was hard to write, but looking back I know it was true.

I did not see them as compromises. I saw opportunities and shot for the stars.

But again, life is full of discoveries. The one thing I know is I love you more than life itself. I would have never made my way off the streets without having you by my side at such a young age. I will forever be grateful, my love, my life, my son.

But this was also a new world for Joshua too. I would be coming home a married man.

He liked Sara and was willing to give her a chance. His mother had him turned on me at such a young age that I always felt I was fighting a battle.

Now, this gorgeous woman was coming home with me and moving into our madhouse, and I needed to change.

Playboy Magazine & Mansion

Life needed to change. About six months into our marriage, Sara was offered to be in Playboy magazine. I had friends who were photographers who said that they wanted her in several different issues. This would be our first time we would have a divide.

She made a bunch of publications and became a cyber girl too. They loved her. But so did Joshua and I. We would even drive to the Playboy Mansion and leave her there for the parties.

Then we picked her up when we were ready to leave, and the divide continued to grow even larger.

The next time she flew to California, I waited at the airport for her, but she never came back home. I went over her phone records and saw she had been talking with a famous television producer. He told her that he was in love with her and she should leave me. I was heartbroken and destroyed.

How could I blame her then?

I was on a roller coaster ride of drugs, parties, patients, and I was half the man I thought that I was. I was nowhere near the man I wanted to become. The man I am today.

Sara eventually did come back home and moved her belongings out. We had a confrontation because I left all of her clothes in the front yard.

Three months passed with Sara living with her girlfriend and her husband.

I was in a dark place and partied even harder. I lost my focus and lost my way. We talked on the phone and decided we wanted to give this another chance.

Once home, we were both torn in different directions again. Sara wanted the fame. I was holding her back. We decided to make a change in life. She offered to give up modeling for Playboy. I offered to give up the nightlife.

It was a sacrifice on both of our parts. But this was a decision we needed to make.

The drugs were the next step we had to kick.

LOSING MY DAD + SARA

Goodbye, Dad

A couple of months later my stepfather passed away. Sara and I were just back from our first anniversary in Hawaii, and my dad had been put in the hospital that same morning. He was transferred to a hospice and died the next day.

I loved my stepfather dearly and got him off of the streets. I did the best I could to help him, but it was his time to go. He made it at home until his last day on Earth.

His family was still multi-millionaires and so too, we thought, was my father.

We were completely wrong.

After all the sucking dry of his trust fund, Jack had close to only $250,000 left to split among his beneficiaries. That included Melissa, Diane, my two nieces, and me. Although Jack had been living with me for close to five years, they never added my son to the trust's beneficiaries.

I was appointed as trustee, and we split the money equally between us. I also asked each person named to give Joshua $5,000 a piece, so he had an inheritance as well. Everyone agreed, even if they did not want to.

They were all expecting millions to be shared. Yet, at the end of the day, we each got just $45,000.

I am so glad I decided to do things in life on my own.

When Melissa and I were young, we always believed that we would be millionaires when Jack passed away, but those dreams were dashed, our father was gone, and we were all left picking up the pieces.

That money, although much smaller than we anticipated, was our family's savior though. The company had gone into debt, and the money came at the right time.

I already refinanced my home to buy the car and invest in the company. And I took out a second mortgage to continue to finance the company too. So, I was at the point where I could not afford my mortgage payments.

I was ashamed and did not want to share this with Sara. I would find a way to make this better.

Sara Leaves Again

But Sara had seen enough of the false hope and unfulfilled promises.

When she left a second time, she took all of the money with her as well as my BMW.

She left my son's money alone though. She loved Joshua and wanted him to have everything. She knew what it was like to go without. So she never wanted him to. She looked at him as a son.

TRUE ROCK BOTTOM

Overdose

When Sara left, I was crushed and decided to go get a hotel room alone.

Then I did an eight ball of cocaine all by myself within three hours.

I should have died.

I almost did.

I might not have realized this at that moment, but it was my first and only attempt at suicide. I was broken and lost and had all but given up.

I was not who I wanted to be, and the drugs masked the simple solution.

Suicide went through my mind throughout my life.

And now I had finally taken the steps so that I might never wake up.

Yet I awoke.

I woke up when my heart started pounding out of my chest. I felt a heart attack coming on. I froze. I did not move.

I prayed to be given a second chance at life and made myself a promise that I would not waste it.

New Promises

I promised I would never do cocaine again.

For real, this time.

I have kept that promise to this day and always will until my last breath.

At that moment, my heart almost stopped. I started doing push-ups, and it sped up again. I rode this near heart attack for about three to four hours.

When it subsided, I went to work with renewed vigor and focus.

I would change and become a better man. No more empty promises.

I would show my wife, my son, and the rest of the world who I was and what I was made of.

This was the moment of transformation for me.

This was an awakening.

I had finally hit rock bottom, and it was only up from here.

PART 7

TRANSFORMATION

GROWTH AND WINNING SARA BACK

Transformation & Growth

I fell to the deepest depths of my mind and soul and came out a better man. I knew I would never do drugs again and have not to this very day.

Was my promise to God? Was it to myself? Was it to my son?

Or was it just a spiritual awakening?

Was I going through some transformation of self-growth?

All I know is it was like a lightbulb going off in my mind. I have never been the same person since that desolate moment.

That moment had the opportunity to end my life, but I used it instead to build one.

I decided I would prove to others what I always knew about myself: I was on my way to greatness.

Here are a few more steps I took forward:

I had already stopped selling marijuana almost a year prior (when my stepfather passed away). And I vowed never to again.

I put all of my focus into my son and my company.

I got my teeth done because I had a messed up, crooked smile.

I worked out daily and lived a good, healthy life.

Life was great. Things were truly turning around.

But something was missing. Someone was missing.

I Need to Get Sara Back

Sara and I had hired lawyers and did not talk for close to six months.

One day, we had a meeting in court in front of the judge with our lawyers. When we saw each other, I just smiled at her. My crooked teeth were now bright, straight, and white.

She had never seen me in a suit, but here I was tanned, in great shape, and, best of all, clean. Clean of any drugs.

I was confident and cocky. I was the man she had fallen in love with again. But a much better version.

I had purchased the other half of my company by paying back the loan, and I no longer took or sold drugs.

My days of struggling were now a thing of the past.

The company had grown exponentially in those six months. My transformation had begun and continued.

If our lawyers had not been so horrendous, we might never have made it through those trying times. But because things were dragged out, we got one final chance.

When we saw one another in the courtroom, the spark was still there.

Sara had met a man during our time apart, but she did not know everything about him. He was a police officer by day but secretly went to gay bars in drag at night.

Just before our court appearance, Sara found out more about him. He had also started asking to wear her undergarments and buy matching high heels.

She had no idea that this officer was leading a double life and realized he wasn't her ideal match.

Picture Complete

With the sparks between us flying again and my finally transforming for the better, I continued to show Sara that I loved her and was there for her.

I always will be there for her.

She is my heart, my rock, and my best friend. She is my better half and helps me see the world through her caring eyes.

She stood by my side when I had nothing to give her except my last name.

I got her back. The picture was finally complete.

WORLD TRAVEL OPENS YOUR EYES

See the World

Over the next few years, Sara and I traveled the world and our company continued to grow. We learned about other cultures and enjoyed each and every discovery together.

We have been blessed to be able to travel all around the world. We both yearn to put our feet in the soft sands of different beaches, breathe the fresh ocean air, and meet new and interesting people.

Every person you ever meet has a story. And we are here to listen and learn.

We enjoy other cultures' customs. You can learn so much about different people from the customs they keep.

And we really enjoy trying new foods in each place we visit. I have eaten everything from alligator, snake, and escargot, to live termites. I ate the termites in Belize and, yes, they really did taste like peppermint.

I even stuck my finger in the hive just like my tour guide did and had a nice little snack.

That was right before we went cave tubing.

What is life without a little bit of travel? We love stepping foot on each and every continent. Life is a journey, and we love to explore all it has to offer.

A Trip of a Lifetime

One of our favorite trips was when we spent a month in Australia, New Zealand, and Fiji. We had booked a trip of a lifetime that came with a tour guide too. Sara and I were excited to visit these destinations.

A few days after we booked the trip, we found out that she was pregnant! We had been trying to get pregnant for five years, so we were elated.

I asked Sara if she wanted to cancel the trip.

She responded, "No, we will ask the doctor. If I'm okay to go and feel able to, then I'd like to go. Who knows when we will ever get the opportunity once the baby is born!"

The doctor gave her permission to leave the country. We were so excited to be able to share this journey, discover new places, and prepare for the arrival of our beautiful little girl.

In all, Sara and I had 18 flights to take. All of this as Sara was getting out of her first trimester. We were about to have a beautiful princess to add to our family.

Joshua, at 18 years old, would finally have the little sister he always wanted.

Was this the same little princess that we saw dancing around on the TV screen four years earlier when we were on mushrooms? Could she materialize right in front of our very eyes?

We felt so much excitement for so many reasons on this trip.

Australia

During our two weeks in Australia, we saw so much. One memorable manmade structure was the Sydney Opera House. How spectacular that was! What an absolute piece of art.

Then, to Uluru in the Outback, we had a champagne toast with all of the Aboriginal people and other guests as the sun set. What a breathtaking and spiritual moment that was.

Watching the sun disappear behind the awe-inspiring background was unforgettable.

The one thing I never expected in the Outback though was all of the camels. Everywhere you looked you saw them! They were just as abundant as the kangaroos.

We found that the Aborigines had chips on their shoulders, but who could blame them? They had their sacred land stripped away from them.

They were not even considered to be humans, or to have any rights as citizens, until 1967. Until then, some were regulated under Flora and Fauna Law (i.e., for plants and animals) and not counted in any state or federal census.

Can you imagine how they were treated?

It reminded me a little bit of my upbringing in feeling unloved, unwanted, and unwelcome so often. We should never make others feel this way.

We also got to travel to the Great Barrier Reef and see all of the magnificent corals and majestic fish. This was one of my favorite moments of my entire life.

To watch the corals sway back and forth in the currents, to see clams as big as Sara and me, and to see the kaleidoscope of colors was truly mesmerizing and life-changing.

We went out to a platform in the middle of the ocean to go snorkeling. This was a couple of years before Sara and I both became Scuba certified. We will go back someday to dive the Great Barrier Reef again, but sadly it will never be the same.

The corals are bleaching at unprecedented rates, and the Crown-of-Thorns Starfish is decimating whatever survives the bleaching. We, as people, need to look back to our oceans and realize that all life starts there. The oceans are so full of beauty and grandeur. They support all life as we know it.

But we humans are destroying the oceans at irreparable rates. I am sad that my children and our future generations will never be able to see the beauty we were able to experience.

They will never see the corals as they flow and breathe.

They may never see all the colors strung together like an unbelievable underwater rainbow.

They may never see the majesty of the Acropora Fields in Australia.

They may never see the density of fish that surround Fiji and the other breathtaking reefs we have visited all around the world.

It truly breaks my heart into thousands of pieces. My love for the ocean runs deep. The ocean and I are one. I feel as if salt water runs through my veins. My toes long to feel the sand beneath them.

Sara and I are even friends with most of the people who run the top public aquariums throughout the United States as well as the top reef tank hobbyists throughout the entire world.

Our passion for the oceans has even made its way into our home and daily life (more on that soon).

New Zealand

Next on our trip, we enjoyed two weeks in New Zealand and got to spend a day with a local family and share a meal with them. The food was amazing. We really enjoyed the natural foods the family grew and produced themselves.

One of the highlights of this part of the trip was when we visited the Māori tribe. All of us tourists were gathered and grouped together. Then they voted one person to become the chief of the tourist tribe.

They voted me the chieftain of our group of guests.

Then, the leader of the Māori tribe and his other tribesman wielded spears, screamed, and rolled their tongues. It was definitely something to remember and behold.

What a terrific show it was. These men were all shirtless and tattooed from head to toe. The whole purpose of this spectacle was to see if they could intimidate you.

You were asked to stay as still as possible, and if you earned their respect, they'd hand you a small fern branch and put their head against yours.

Once both of your heads touched, you, in turn, would share a breath.

Once a breath is shared, you and your people are welcomed into their tribe. You then share a meal and dance around. You are, in turn, one with them. You are welcomed into their home, and they wish you the best on your journey of life.

I have always looked back and found this such a kind gesture of harmony and peace. You go from all of that anger and intimidation to peace and harmony in one single breath.

I wish the whole world were this way. I wish that the problems of the world could be resolved by taking one long deep breath. I believe it can be if we all share in the breath as one.

This was one of the highlights of our magnificent vacation.

Departing from this experience with the Māori tribe, we then went on to travel around other spots in New Zealand.

We had the chance to see Christchurch not too long after the earthquake in 2011. We saw all the horrific damage that was caused. There were ruins of buildings and homes scattered everywhere. The people were left to pick up the pieces of what was left of their lives.

The destruction was real, and our trip there was short.

Fiji

Next up was Fiji. The three days we spent there were majestic and mesmerizing. I fell in love with the island that we were on: Denarau.

Once you arrive, you cannot believe your eyes.

I thought we would meet a lot of native Islanders, but everywhere you looked you saw Indian people who had relocated to the islands. Turbans as far as your eyes could see.

I can tell you that traveling opens up your eyes and changes your whole perception of the world as well.

You start out with a preconceived notion about a destination, but once you arrive, it can be entirely different.

Take Australia and the camels, for example. I would have never of guessed it. Or the rabbit problem in New Zealand. Rabbits were brought there to kill the pests but became an even bigger problem themselves.

Life always throws you a little mystery to keep things interesting.

The Sofitel Fiji Resort, where we stayed, took us out snorkeling on my birthday and I was surrounded by thousands of beautiful fish. They handed me a loaf of bread and said, "Enjoy."

And that is what I did.

I stood alongside the reef. The water was about six feet deep and very warm. It almost felt as if you were in a bath. The marine life was colorful and abundant.

The fish swam right up and surrounded me. Hundreds of them ate from my hands. I had found my little piece of paradise. I found my Zen and enjoyed every single fish.

I felt as if I were surrounded by more beautiful fish than I could even imagine. I had Clownfish, Tangs, Angels, Parrot Fish, and Groupers to name a few.

Some moments are ingrained in one's mind and last a lifetime. This was one of those times for me.

This moment makes me smile even as I write about it now.

I will always remember this moment and hold it close to my heart. The majesty of the ocean always wins me over and takes my breath away.

I have had a love for the ocean as early as I can remember. I believe my parents took us a couple of times when we were very young, and that's when my love affair started.

Europe, the Caribbean, South & Central America, and Beyond

Where else have we traveled?

We've had the pleasure of visiting many places all over Europe (Rome and Paris stand out in my mind), all over the Caribbean, and also magical places like Brazil, Costa Rica, Panama, Belize, and Honduras.

Traveling to new locations with different languages, foods, cultures, and customs is an excellent education about others and even about yourself.

Put travel at the top of your list.

CREMATING MY MOM

Goodbye, Mom

My mother passed away when we were in Australia.

The drugs finally caught up to her.

Over the years we saw her clean, then doing hard drugs, then drinking, then taking pills, and back to the hard drugs again. It was a never-ending vicious cycle until it finally ended when she mixed medications and did not wake up.

When we got home from our trip, the first thing we did was have my mother cremated. Sara and I had a small reception for our immediate family too.

The reception was a celebration of life, and we talked about all of the good and even the bad.

It was tough being gone for a whole month and right in the middle of it finding out your mother had passed away, but we tried to make the best of it.

You are left lonely and helpless. You are left with so many questions that will never be answered.

"Mom, did you kill yourself?"

"Was it a mistake?"

My wife shed tears right alongside me for many days straight.

It made us very sad to know that my mother would never see our daughter's beautiful smile or to hear her deep laugh. My mother would never see Joshua grow into the great man he is today.

All memories and possibilities were ripped from her as she took pills that did not mix well together and never woke up. This whirlwind of hot and cold that I had called mom was finally laid to rest.

She had the pain of 10 lifetimes rolled up into one. Actually, I could not believe she had lived as long as she had, but that did not take away the guilt that I had and have felt.

I felt as if I had let her down by not answering her calls (at 3 AM Australian time) while my wife and I were traveling. The time difference impeded my ability to help walk her through all of her problems or talk her down from her deep depression.

Depression had finally taken hold, and she had no one there for her.

Melissa and our mother were fighting so she could not turn to my little sister either.

Eli and mom did not have much of a relationship because he had seen the drugs and abuse and stayed as far away from that drama as he possibly could.

My mother's trials were hers alone on that sad and lonely final day.

James was probably out gambling or begging for spare change as he had on and off for the last 30 years.

I could not talk her down or bring her back. But I believe that she is now set free. Free of all of her pain. Her demons are finally vanquished.

Butterfly

My mother used to say that when she died, she wanted to come back as a butterfly in Butterfly World in Florida.

I believe that she now smiles down on us as the woman that she once was.

As her wings flutter about, she makes sure all is good in our worlds.

She is the Gypsy who we knew and loved.

I still see her dancing and twirling around in my dreams.

I even saw her in a dream and had to tell her that she had passed away. She was in disbelief, crying and begging me to tell her it was not true.

The lost little girl who was my mom is now a guardian angel to my daughter and my son.

I believe she had so much love to give but was lost in all the pain that she experienced throughout her lonely and sad life.

I believe she did not have the strength to handle all of her inner pain and turmoil on her own.

But I believe she lives on in my children.

I see the good and the bad all rolled into each and every one of her children and our children.

Signs from Above

I think about my mother all of the time, and sometimes I get glimpses that she is still with us.

One of the last memories I had with her was at the three-dimensional ultrasound when we saw our daughter for the very first time. She called Sara "Little Mama," and it stuck.

My mother promised to be in the hospital when my wife gave birth, and we believe, even though she passed away, she was there with us.

From the hospital bed, Sara and I were saying how we wished mom was there and looked up at the clock on the wall at that very moment and the minute hand began to spin.

It spun around hour after hour. I took it off of the wall, and it was battery operated.

No one has been able to tell me otherwise. Mom, I know you were there and thank you and love you for it. You will always have a place in my heart.

Another sign you are watching over us was when your favorite song came on the radio while they were taking a picture of the butterfly tattoo I had just gotten.

You are still with us.

I believe that when you do good in the world, you see more of these signs that those you love are watching over you and guiding you down the right path.

DEATH OF MY BIOLOGICAL FATHER

Goodbye, Pops

My biological father Peter died not too long after my mother. Both of them much too young to die.

Yet, somehow they lived much longer than they both possibly should have.

My Pops had a heart attack and was found a couple of days later with a doorknob clenched in his hand.

He died lonely and alone.

Maybe his mind traveled back to Mars and he found his peace. Or maybe, just maybe, he is still here with me looking over my shoulder along with my mother, stepfather, Gma, and Sister.

Death is inevitable, and we all have to look mortality in the face.

I do not want to die this way.

PATH FOR GOOD IS FINALLY CLEAR

The Good Path

My path is finally clear.

For so long I struggled to find my way and get past survival mode to flourish mode where I can give back to others and give back to the world, more purposefully.

I am finally on the right path, and so is our business and team.

Our company Precision Orthotics & Prosthetics (POP) likes to positively change lives.

We strive to make a difference in the community and help make the world a better place.

To give you more details on what we do, we work closely with physicians to help clients with their orthotic needs.

This includes bracing needs like cranial remolding helmets and scoliosis braces. And also compression needs to help minimize muscle aches, reduce swelling, and support the internal function of the veins.

And our prosthetics help amputees who have lost anything from fingers to limbs.

We also help diabetic patients with specific feet and limb issues too.

Our work directly and positively impacts those who need it most.

Jimmy Colson

A Business Can Help More People, Beyond Yourself and Your Family

Having a healthy, thriving business not only supports our family, but it also helps us to be able to give back to our patients and our community.

For example, we have made prosthetic legs for cancer patients at no charge to them, just because they couldn't afford it.

I will never forget the face on this 17-year-old young lady when I told her she would not need to pay for her new leg. That we would be doing it free of charge. The cost to her? Nothing more than a smile.

As the tears flowed and her smile got bigger, I had a moment of clarity.

We are doing our part in this beautiful world.

All of our good deeds make a difference for the hurting and the underprivileged.

Recently, we donated over 150 pairs of shoes to a homeless shelter. These people cannot afford shoes, but now wear brand new ones to protect their feet.

The feeling that wells up when you know you are making a positive difference is well worth all effort and any expense to my fantastic crew of practitioners and me.

My team makes me proud every day.

I'm proud of the compassion our staff shows for others. Proud to call them part of our family. The POP family. We have done charity work on many occasions to extend our hands out beyond our family to other families too.

We sponsor underprivileged families every year to make sure their children do not experience childhoods like ours.

We love seeing the smiles on these kids' faces when they receive the gifts that we have gotten just for them (that they get to keep and do not have to watch get taken back for money to buy drugs).

The parents' faces almost top the children's! They are grateful, gracious, and delighted at the sight of joy in their kids.

We also donate to numerous cancer foundations and give our time whenever we can.

What is life if you are not making a positive difference for others?

It is wasted.

Focus on the positive. Do good. Even if it is just one small thing, for one person at a time.

And if you have acquired skills as a hustler, as I did, then you are an entrepreneur too.

Read, learn, and study more skills to help you in business.

It is an incredible way to help yourself, your family, your clients, your community, and the world.

POSITIVE RECOGNITION

It Feels Good to Do Good

I am honored to say that even others have recognized the positive impact that Sara and I have sought to bring into the world.

Here are a few proud moments for us.

1. "Top 100 Most Influential Men of the Year" in Las Vegas

I was voted one of the most influential men in Las Vegas in 2015. I believe they chose me because of all we do for our patients and in our industry. I was beyond flattered and extremely proud of this designation.

And I was the only man who added a picture of not just himself but also his wife when they asked for a headshot. I believe I was only half the man that I am today back when I met Sara. She deserved to be in the publication with me as well.

2. Sara Was Named "Mastectomy Fitter of the Year"

And I am so proud of my wife. When her aunt (and godmother) was diagnosed with breast cancer many years ago, Sara decided she wanted to do more to help women all over the world.

So, she studied with American Breast Care, completed 1,500 clinical hours, and passed an exam to become an American Board Certified Mastectomy Fitter.

What is that?

It is a healthcare professional who helps the physicians who work with patients post-mastectomy who have had breast cancer.

Sara is trained to make custom breast forms (that match the patient's skin tone, freckles, moles, and even veins), properly fit them, and adjust external breast prostheses, bras, and related supplies to help with the physical and emotional well-being of patients.

The forms we make are so lightweight that our patients do not even feel like they are wearing anything.

In 2015, Sara was honored as the Mastectomy Fitter of the Year.

3. Congressional Recognition

We received congressional recognition for the humanitarian work we did in sponsoring underprivileged children of ethnicity all around Las Vegas.

We have bought everything from washers and dryers, to computers, to bikes and beds. We do whatever we can to make a difference in each and every life we come across.

I cannot tell you how great doing good feels.

A CALL TO POSITIVE ACTION

Don't Waste Your Chance

Why waste the platform you have?

Why not speak up and make the change that you want to see for others?

Shout from the mountain tops and inspire others to do better, to be better. As Gandhi once said, "Be the change that you want to see in the world."

We have more power than we know.

A simple smile might make someone's day. Kind words might change someone's life.

Make sure you continue to grow.

With growth, you can aid others with your words and actions.

If you get anything from this book, I hope it is to trust in yourself and be a better version of you each and every day.

I am not perfect, nor will I ever be. But what I am is someone who wishes you the best. I wish you the best that life has to offer. I wish that when you get your opportunity, that you take it and accomplish great things.

I wish that we all can leave our imprint and turn this world around.

Let's make it a better place each and every day.

Believe

Believe, my friends.

Believe in love and dreams.

Believe in your heart and imagine the world that you want to live in and make it your very own. Help make it happen.

I believe in you and your dreams.

I believe that you will accomplish great things and can be more and do more. You are never too old to become who you might have been. I have always believed that with all of my heart.

If you continue to grow, you can conquer your fears and slay your demons. If you continue to believe, you will silence your critics and make the difference that you seek.

Never give up hope. Do not become a number or just a memory.

Become the best version of *you* and look your fears head-on. You can do amazing things.

The hardest thing to do is taking that first step.

And the first step is believing in yourself when you feel no one else will. The first step is owning your qualities and flaws and knowing that you can make a difference.

You will be a difference maker.

Life is too short to waste it.

Take Positive Action Forward

I hope that my words ring in your ears and make you think.

A simple thought is all it takes to start an action. That action can spark something deep inside you that cannot be contained: a fire that can grow, consume you, and guide you on your path to greatness.

Hope is one thing that no one can take away from you.

As long as you have hope and a dream, you have a chance!

And as long as you stay on course and build your way to greatness, it becomes your destiny.

When you leave this world, how do you want to be remembered?

How do you want your family and friends to feel at your passing?

Do right by them.

Do right by everyone.

Make sure that your actions are genuine and your heart is pure. If you live with these two rules, you will accomplish great things.

PART 8

LESSONS LEARNED

LIFE LESSONS

Focus on Solutions

Life is full of encounters with people who have problems but do not want to find solutions.

We all have those family members or friends who are never happy with where they are, who they are, or where they are going in life. Those people are the ones whose wheels are always spinning, but they are getting nowhere fast.

They are the people who always have an opinion but once you give yours, they look at you with their ears covered and their minds closed. They look at you with a blank stare as you try to extend your hand and help them along their journey.

The problem with being compassionate in all that you do is you will pick up lost souls along the way and always want to help them to better themselves. You want to fix everyone and everything.

It can be a blessing and a curse.

Sure, you are trying to positively change lives, but you need to keep in mind that if those people do not help themselves, they will continue using you and riding your coattails until you too are empty.

The hardest part in all of this is when you come to the conclusion that these lost souls are actually bringing the problems upon themselves.

Some people cheat throughout life and wonder why they cannot find love. They do not understand why the people they choose do not love them, yet they never give others one hundred percent.

Others lie and steal and wonder why no one trusts them.

They wonder why they have no job, why they have no future, and yet still have no plans to change their shady ways.

They go on in life feeling sorry for themselves, yet never look in the mirror to realize that they are the problem.

Lying, cheating, and stealing will always lead you down a dangerous path. Bad karma is something you cannot escape.

I find it funny and ironic that when people constantly complain, they do not see that the answers to all of their questions are actually right in front of them. All you need to do is take that first step in growth.

You need to open your eyes and your mind will follow.

Change is Good

The only way to achieve what you want in this world is to change.

Change can be subtle or extreme.

Change your thoughts and your actions will follow.

Change your perspective and you see the world differently.

After all, you can see much better from a mountaintop than from any valley. You can begin your climb at any time.

If you are always sad, figure out what makes you smile and that is the start to being happy. Think happy thoughts, give compliments, and enjoy how the view starts to change.

Depression is horrible and affects many of us, including myself. I sometimes get depressed even if everything in the world seems amazing.

Sometimes the beginning of our moods is beyond our control. But we choose how we react and can take ahold of them to have better days ahead.

If you are gaining too much weight, try to watch what you eat (or even write it down to simply track it) and see the positive results start to arrive.

We all can be caught up binge eating when things are not going right. Put down the ice cream and the soda and open your eyes.

We need to control our actions.

If you do binge eat, follow it up with a nice walk. Try to stay active.

In my profession, we see the results of so many people who let themselves go. Diabetes is one of the most dangerous words that you can hear. I have seen numerous people lose their limbs because of this horrible disease.

So many people who do not take care of themselves lose their lives.

In my profession, we also enjoy a lot of happy outcomes. We may see a child walk for the first time or a veteran get back on his or her feet, literally.

But when you lose a patient, especially to something within their control, a part of you dies as well.

It can be hard giving your heart and soul to your patients. But I could not live any other way.

Sometimes things are beyond our power, but sometimes we can avoid disaster by looking at our trials in the face and standing up to them.

If you believe it, you can achieve it.

If you are in a bad relationship — or in a string of bad relationships — look inside yourself, and you may realize that you are broken too.

Maybe you are half of the problem and need to change in order to attract and keep the right person in your life.

I have always found broken people and tried to fix them, or at least help them to fix themselves. I have done that in all aspects of life. From finding women who were physically or verbally abused to finding friends with no homes and taking them in.

I took in so many friends off of the streets in my younger years that I can no longer do it.

I see so many talented people giving up before they even begin. So many people have the skills to better their lives but do not have the determination or hunger to make it all work.

Try to find your inner fire and build from there. If you are passionate about something, you can give it your all. You can do big, important things if you believe in yourself.

If you don't, who else will?

Who else will give you a chance when you cannot hold your chin up and be proud of yourself?

Confidence shines through. Good deeds do as well.

If you do good for others, they will want to watch you grow. The more people you bring up with you, the higher you can catapult up too. So always be happy when someone else gets ahead.

You don't lose when others win.

We all win.

They are giving you new ideas or new blueprints for how you and others can do the same.

We all learn differently and grow at different rates. As long as you are always trying to take a step forward, you will end up being who you always wanted to become.

Treat Others Kindly, Learn from Everyone

Make sure you leave such a positive lasting impression that people seek you out. Do right by everyone, and others will want to help you. This enables you to start to grow your network.

Networks can be built strong with people from all walks of life.

You never know when the mailman or the server at the fast food establishment might have the keys to unlock your next idea. They might be waiting for a chance to grow and make a difference too.

So many people make the mistake of thinking certain people are beneath them.

Those who have an open mind are the ones who will ascend to greater heights.

Always keep your mind open.

We all have a thirst for knowledge. It is always rewarding and surprising when you learn something new from someone you would never have thought could teach you.

The best teacher is life experience. Because of this, I love having conversations with older people. They have so much to teach.

Children do too; I learn the most from them. They see the world through unjaded eyes. They have beautiful minds and hearts.

Their souls are pure.

My daughter Liliana is always teaching me and making me smile. She keeps my wife and me on our toes.

Find people in your life you can learn from, be inspired by, and inspire in return.

PRINCESS LILIANA

Our Princess

Since both Sara and I grew up really poor, we decided to spoil our little "Princess Liliana" once she entered our world.

We agreed that as long as she always stayed appreciative, polite, humble, and generous that we would give her the best childhood humanly possible.

But the first thing we did was make sure that she learned impeccable manners.

I did the same for Joshua, and he has always had a kind heart, holds doors open for ladies, and is a true gentleman. Sara says she fell in love with me because of how well-mannered Joshua was when we met.

Liliana has a heart of gold too and gives away so many of her toys and treasures to help homeless children. She looks at everyone — like Sara and I do — with no judgment.

She believes that there is good in everyone.

Everyone deserves a chance to prove that they deserve more and that they can be more.

Our beautiful little girl is also an old soul.

You can see her wisdom and beauty hidden behind her kaleidoscope blue eyes.

Both of my children are old souls who see the world through different sets of eyes.

Joshua can see the good and bad in people. He is a realist but is very in tune with what is going on around the world and in the community.

Liliana looks through rose-colored glasses. She sees the good in everyone and everything.

So even though they are both old souls, each sees the world so much differently.

An interesting similarity between the two of them is around birthdays. Joshua never liked when we sang him *Happy Birthday*. He would get embarrassed and cry.

Liliana is the same way. We cannot sing *Happy Birthday* to her, or she will want to run away from the party. So we only sing to her when immediate family are present.

Four Special Things

So, here are four fun, unique things we've enjoyed doing so far for Liliana:

1. Castle Bedroom
The first part of spoiling our princess was making her a castle bedroom. We had a custom two-floor bed built. The top level has stairs leading up to it and a slide coming down.

The second, lower story where her bed is also has a television and DVD player. She has had the bed since she was two years old.

2. Disney Princess Paintings
The second part was painting her playroom with all of the Disney princesses. It is a beautiful piece of art. All of the princesses look over her as Liliana and her friends play.

3. Cool Kid's Pool
The third step was building a second pool. We have two pools in our backyard. One is Sara's and my pool which has a water screen, brass dolphins that shoot water into the pool, a movie screen that is 220 inches, and a waterfall grotto that also has flames that rise from it.

The second pool is for Princess Liliana and pals. She has a grotto and a waterfall with a rock slide. Her friends are always over going from pool to pool. They jump off of the waterfalls, zip down the slides, and have all out water fights.

4. The Rabbit Hole
The fourth thing is what we call the Rabbit Hole. We have a private basement hidden behind a bookcase that is fully painted in Alice in Wonderland decor.

Once the door is opened, you see the white rabbit ready to dive down the rabbit hole. He has his clock in hand. I'm sure he was late for a very important date.

To your left, you have my wife's collection of Alice memorabilia and the whole tea party scene painted with bright pastel colors. I think it truly is a breathtaking sight.

Straight in front of you, you see the Cheshire cat smiling with different colored lights that alternate.

On your right, you have Alice being poured upwards from a teacup.

Sara and Liliana often sit on the steps and enjoy the views.

But the best part is at the bottom of the stairwell. There you have a full-on arcade and a three-level movie theater with reclining chairs. Once children end up down there, they never want to leave.

We spend a lot of our family time down in this play area for adults and kids alike.

Parenting

But even with all of these gifts, it has not changed Liliana for the worse. They have actually made her even more generous and understanding. Parenting is a tough job. There is no right or wrong way of going about it.

Just as long as you provide your children the two things that they deserve the most: your love and your time.

Children need that one-on-one time with their parents. Liliana is closing in on seven years old as I write this and we have never spent a night away from her.

We may be overprotective, but she is happy, and I will take that each and every time over a sad, little princess. Our number one job is to let our children know they are loved and cared for.

No one gave us a map or a guide for how to parent the right way.

So it is in our power to make the best memories and also give the best childhood to our amazing children that we can. Ones Sara and I didn't quite have.

Kids are the future.

Let's teach them right from wrong and let them come up with their own opinions and beliefs for the next generation.

Let's give them hope where there might not be any.

Let's broaden their imaginations and teach them to dream big.

Let's give this world the future leaders it needs.

I wish I had what I do today when my son was born. But that was a different world. One where we slept on floors and took buses around town.

I believe that it is hard on a parent realizing that you are a completely different person at 45 compared to 25.

But it does not make you love either child any more or any less.

Life is all about growth, and I have been blessed with a career that has enabled me to grow professionally, spiritually, and emotionally.

REEF TANKS: A HEALTHY ADDICTION

How My Healthy Addiction Grew

I spend one day a week taking care of all seven of our aquariums.

In the fish tank community (my favorite hobby) you have all different types of people.

You have those who want a couple of Nemo fish or a Dory fish and don't even know the difference between saltwater or freshwater. All they know is they want a fish and they try to figure it all out on the fly.

You also have those who try hard to grow coral or keep fish, but give up at the first sign of failure or the first sign of any trouble at all. They look at the dollar signs that it will take to replace the fish or coral, and run.

You also have the guys like my friends and me with full-on addictions. My addictions were bad in my younger years: drugs, drinking, women, partying, and fighting. Those times were trying on me both physically and mentally.

But with my new, healthier addiction I am able to maintain my very own ecosystem and help make it thrive.

Now my addiction is adding coral and fish to our beautiful reef aquariums.

When I initially got into aquariums, I was making $10 an hour and wanted a reef tank more than anything in the entire world. I had aquariums with freshwater fish, but a *reef* was nothing more than a pipe dream.

Being from California and also having lived in Maui, I fell in love with the ocean. Yet all the fish I had ever had to date were freshwater and originated in lakes and rivers. I had raised Oscars and African Cichlids. I dabbled in Jack Dempsey's and Convicts.

But reefing was the next level.

The chemistry and all the different things you need to balance for a successful reef are insane. The challenge is real and it is fun.

The fish-only freshwater tanks are aggressive, and there is some challenge to it, but you only have to worry about waste in the tank and feeding the fish. The freshwater fish eat and breed. Then you have the same thing happen the very next day. That's about it. The challenge and upkeep are minimal.

That's nothing compared to reef keeping. It is like the difference between checkers and chess.

With saltwater reef tanks, you see something different every time you look into your tank.

FROM THE DEPTHS

Back in 1995, I decided to use my first bonus check from work to purchase a reef tank. I have been hooked ever since.

In the earlier days of reefing, we were all learning as we went. We would add fish that did not stand a chance of living in captivity without special instructions. We would try to put corals in that had special care, but none of us knew what that was back then. We figured it out and then learned about the next fish or coral.

We used filtration like under gravel filters or fluidized beds that always had deep sand beds. The filters would suck the muck under the gravel only to have problems once our tanks matured. And the lighting was atrocious. We had big bulbs that never gave enough light to sustain coral. (All big no-no's.)

But we tried, we learned, and we progressed.

As the hobby grew, so did the technology. Those under gravel filters would soon turn into tanks full of seaweed (called Caulerpa or Chaeto), underneath the tank, in a tank of their own.

We had problems with nitrates and phosphates, but then along came protein skimmers. They spin and form a foam (like the waves do in the ocean) to remove fish waste.

Then the lighting went from bulbs to Metal Halide, to T5, and now we run our tanks off of LED lighting. The LED lighting helps keep the tanks cooler, thus making a lot of the chillers dispensable.

(We all had to have chillers cool our tanks before LEDs to keep the temperature in check. You never want your reef tank hovering over 80 degrees.)

Back in the earlier days of my reef keeping adventure, I had an apartment, an older vehicle, a big screen TV (that I got from a rent-to-own place), and a reef tank. This was dead in the middle of the ghetto where I called home.

I could barely afford my bills, but when a new coral or fish came out, I jumped at it.

I also met great people doing this hobby, including Brett and Wayde from Animal Planet's TV show *Tanked*. They were in the early stages of building their empire, and I was in there every day buying a new coral or fish from them.

The Big Tank & Reef Party

This year — in 2018 — we had the Marine Aquarium Conference of North America (MACNA) come to Las Vegas for their 30-year anniversary show.

Sara and I threw a party in our home and were blessed to have people from all around the world wanting to join us to see our amazing reef tank (one will be on an episode we filmed for *Tanked*)!

The party was unbelievable.

We had over 400 hundred people show up from Japan, Germany, England, Holland, Italy, Australia, Fiji, and so many different islands that I would run out of room to name them all here.

The vibe was great with people mingling from all corners of the globe. We had people who ran the largest aquariums in the world, divers, professors, and marine biologists everywhere. Some tables had multiple Aquarists of the Year mingling and sharing stories, each person wanting nothing more than to save the world's reefs.

And, for fun, we had Elvis singing, showgirls walking around, delicious food being served by three chefs, and an open bar. People competed in our arcade to earn bragging rights on who was the best player on each game.

It was one of the most memorable nights ever.

Life is all about sharing and giving back. This was a way I felt we could give back to the hobby that I truly love. We could show our appreciation for our friends and family.

And when you have someone come up to you from Australia to let you know that the almost 30,000 tanks around the world he has seen have been leading him up to ours?

He said it was the nicest aquarium he had ever seen in his life.

Or, to have one of the biggest exporters of coral from Fiji call my tank Noah's Ark?

Wow, I was humbled and felt truly blessed.

We also had people from Japan do a piece on our tank that they will publish in a Japanese magazine.

I felt so proud and accomplished. I actually felt as if I belonged in this incredible hobby. I went from a man with no high school education to someone who can grow a whole underwater reef in my own living room.

A boy with little hope became a man who tries to inspire and *give* hope.

Will Our Love Live On?

A few of the top exporters of coral in the world were in our home for the party, and I saw them shed a tear. Why? It was bittersweet. They appreciated the beauty of my tanks but were also saddened by the loss our world is experiencing.

Mine is one of the last of the spectacular reef tanks because all the corals are being banned from collections. Our hobby will soon be a thing of the past. People will never get to experience this majesty ever again because the coral reefs are dying.

But, with the help of friends of mine, we hope that the reefs will regenerate someday. I have friends who replant corals on the reefs to give them a chance to regrow and thrive.

Let's hope and pray that this works.

Let's hope that our grandchildren will someday get to experience the ocean as we have.

It is a dream that we all hope to see come true. We long to experience a rebirth and to watch the oceans regenerate. But as the ocean temperatures change, so does the ecosystem.

We reef keepers are trying to find ways to save the reefs — some are learning about coral spawning and others are breeding rare fish — but it is up to all of us to care for our planet and oceans.

Our Tanks

Sara and I have had tanks of all sizes and dimensions, but our current one is the crown jewel. It is 600 gallons with another 500-gallon tank right underneath the main display tank, where I grow all of my seaweed and have other corals and fish breeding and propagating.

I have had tube tanks, small nano tanks, 500-gallon cube tanks, and a lot of success over the years. But this tank has taken my heart and soul.

We reefers have to have patience because corals take years to grow and fill in. I believe this has helped me in other aspects of life too. To grow, maintain, and sustain a reef you must put your heart into it. I do that in all aspects of my life. I lead with my heart and see where it takes me.

I feel so accomplished when I see my coral grow from a ½-inch fragment into a 2-foot healthy piece that is thriving.

My aquariums are a labor of love.

In addition to the 1100-gallon reef system, Liliana has a 90-gallon seahorse tank with soft corals and slow fish, and Sara has the 350-gallon cylinder tank that we just filmed for our TV episode. But these tanks do not even say it all. I also have a 40-gallon tank in our guest house, two quarantine tanks in our fish room, and a cylinder and reef tank at my Las Vegas office.

I used to have others help me with the aquariums, but now I try to do as much as I can myself. It takes a lot of time, love, and patience but every drop of blood, sweat, or tears is worth it to see my reefs thrive.

Ocean Life is Amazing!

I hope we as people learn to love our oceans and the life within it before it is too late. The ocean has more colors of coral and fish than any of us could possibly imagine.

For example, the beauty of the Mandarin Goby is unparalleled in nature. The intricate lines and colors are mesmerizing.

And the bright, vivid colors of Purple Tilefish or the deep reds of Hawaii Flame Wrasses are just stunning.

Fish can also use disguise, which is so cool. Take for example the Anglers who use camouflage to eat unsuspecting prey.

Or Wrasses, they flash their finnage to display themselves better to attract or to deter other fish.

You have fish that bury themselves in the sand, others that wedge themselves in the rocks, and still others that hitch rides on bigger fish.

There's so much diversity in the ocean!

And if you think that fish are interesting, you will not believe how diverse corals are. Most people think corals are plants, but they are not. Corals are animals.

And there are many different kinds of corals like:
- Small Polyp Stony corals (SPS are my favorite)
- Large Polyp Stony corals (LPS have hard skeletons, but the feeders are soft)
- Soft corals like Zoanthids and leather corals

Corals come in all shapes, sizes, and colors, and they can propagate or reproduce only in the right conditions.

I can say one thing about all of these beautiful animals and that is I would not be where I am in life without finding a hobby I could be so passionate about. A hobby that makes me think, focus, and care. A hobby that can pull my mind away from running a large company and help me escape from the daily grind.

I am blessed to know the best reefers from all around the world now. I thank each of them for sharing their knowledge, a helping hand, and most of all their friendship with Sara and me.

Find Your Healthy Addiction

You need not love the ocean like I do to gain a deeper level of life satisfaction. You might love to hike, ride bikes, or camp. We all need a release from the everyday monotony.

I chose reef keeping.

Think of what you choose and put your heart into it. Work hard to save up for that nice bike. Or maybe you want a hot rod race car. If you cannot afford it now, set your goals with a timeline for when you will be able to afford it.

Life is so much better with dreams and goals.

We all need something to shoot for. Start small and the momentum will build into a self-fulfilling prophecy of achieving your lofty goals. Set goals, take action to achieve them, get closer, take more action, achieve your goals, set new ones, etc.

Once I achieve my goals, I set higher ones.

Turn your dreams and aspirations into milestones you work toward making real. The only thing that will ever hold you back in this abundant world is yourself. Do not come up with excuses. Come up with solutions.

Never defame anyone. True colors always shine through. If you pay attention and look for clues and cues, people are so transparent that you can see their next move before it is even made.

Life is such a beautiful journey that you need to choose wisely who you want to join you on this fantastic ride.

Your inner circle of friends will either lift you up to unseen heights or bring you crashing back down to the darkest depths.

So, lift one another out of the stratosphere. Aid others in this wonderful journey of discovery, and you might even have a few people shooting for the stars, just like you.

THE NEXT CHAPTER

So Can You

As I write this, I have reached my multi-millionaire goal. Who would have thought that possible for a kid like me with a life like mine? Nothing is out of your reach. Trust me. I always pinch myself and hope that I never wake from this unbelievable dream. I know how blessed I really am. I will always be grateful and stay humble.

I now want to double our revenue within the next 10 years. I know that sounds crazy but without lofty goals, greatness is unobtainable.

But believe me, it isn't about the money. It's about the impact. It's about showing the world that any lost child with hope and dreams can accomplish whatever they set their minds to. If you believe, you can truly achieve every dream your heart desires.

No one believed in me. But I am here to tell you that I do believe in *you*!

I believe in your hopes and dreams. I believe that you have the potential to leave a positive impact on this world.

Now it is time for you to believe in yourself too.

Coming up for me, I also want to do more public speaking to share more stories and inspiration with people of all ages, but especially young adults and teenagers who are going through tough struggles and do not see the light out yet.

I made it out and so can you!

A FINAL NOTE TO MY FAMILY

To Joshua

Joshua, you gave me hope when I had none.

You gave me a purpose in life, and I strived for greatness just to show you that it was possible.

You are an incredible young man.

Believe in yourself. I believe in you.

I always have and always will.

To Liliana

You have greatness within you, Liliana, my mini. I want you to know that you brought out the best in me and I am eternally grateful and have learned so much from you.

The best gift you have given me is to see the world through your beautiful blue eyes.

You will also make a positive difference in this wonderful world. You have the most beautiful heart that I have ever seen. You make me smile each and every day.

I cannot wait to see what the world has in store for you, Princess.

Greatness is in your future.

To Sara

Sara, my beautiful wife, the universe brought you into my life for a reason. And I am happy to see our marriage grow, as does my love for you as the mother of our beautiful princess and as such an amazing wife.

You truly have a beautiful heart of gold and will always be my best friend. You stood by my side when I did not have anything except a crooked smile and a little charisma. I want you to know that this means everything to me.

You are my rock.

I thank you for being a major part of this journey with me.

We both have gone from poor children from broken homes to multi-millionaire business owners, receiving congressional recognition for all that we do within our community.

And we are just getting started.

**The three of you amaze and complete me.
I love you with all of my heart and soul.**

A FINAL NOTE TO YOU

Dear Reader

In closing, I'd love to share with you a few more reflections on what I have taken away from my trials, tribulations, and transformation.

This entire book, including the remainder of this section, has been written just for you.

I wanted to show you that no matter the depths, there is light above if you keep swimming in the right direction and never give up.

Reflection on Hope

Never give up hope. Hope is all that you need.

Get rid of the drama that haunts your life. Realizing who helps you to grow and who hinders your growth is paramount. Believe that each day will be better than your last.

You are responsible for your own self-worth.

You cannot depend on others to get you to the place you strive to get to. Only you can get to where you are able to watch and enjoy every goal and dream coming true.

That falls on your shoulders and yours alone.

Without believing in yourself, no one else will believe in you either.

Reflection on Marriage

Remember, my friends, all marriages have struggles and trials. Nothing and no one is ever perfect. It is human nature to either grow together or to grow apart. It is our job as spouses and parents to make an effort to aid our families in their journey of growth.

Marriage should never be taken lightly.

If you loved your spouse enough to marry them, they should be worth the time and effort to protect them and to nurture the love that you have for one another.

Blame is the easiest thing to give. But it is also the hardest thing to accept.

Owning your flaws and faults will help you transform into the person you have always wanted to become. You can always become a better person.

Therefore, love your spouse as much as you love yourself. If you do not love yourself, then that should be your very first step.

How can anyone love you if you do not know self-love?

How can you give your heart to anyone until you are whole?

I can let you know when I saw my wife's heart fill completely. I had seen love in her eyes before, but the moment she held our beautiful daughter for the first time is ingrained in my mind and heart eternally.

I watched the tears fall and witnessed her grow into the person I always knew she would become. That was five years into our marriage, watching our Liliana May being born.

Sara went through terrible pain during labor, but we got to leave the hospital with the most beautiful gift in this world. I thank her for changing my life for the better. I thank her for sticking by my side when I was nothing more than half of a man.

We are very blessed to be a team and try to make a difference in this world together. Even if that difference is one person at a time. All of the trials we have faced made us stronger, and I love Sara more each and every day.

Reflection on Children

Our children are a reflection of what they see.

If they see fighting, we wire them to fight.

If they see a relationship with no love, that will be what they seek out.

If they hear names being called, they will call names.

I struggled with each of the above throughout my life. These were hard habits to break. We are all a continual work-in-progress, and I still make mistakes.

But as you see in these memoirs, I own them. My mistakes are mine and mine alone. I would not be the person I am today without the good and the bad.

I just try to be a better version of myself.

I saw the worst things possible in relationships and somehow always fell into the same problems. It was as if I were reliving the same relationship with each woman I met. I had to recognize that, own it, and grow from it.

I could not love anyone because I did not know how to love myself.

That was before I knew I had to make a life change.

Sara had to make a life change as well. Our number one job in this life is to be the best parents we can be for our beautiful children. We are here to leave our legacy of amazing people who can help change this world for the better.

Reflection on This Book

Legacy and change: that is what this book is about. It is not about wealth. It is about inner peace. It is about spiritual awakenings and growth of all kinds. This book is about dreaming big and doing what you believe is right.

It is about knowing you are not perfect and that you do not have to be. The only thing I can teach you is to try to be a better version of you.

If I can accomplish that, for even one of you, I have succeeded. My goal for writing this book and letting you know my deepest and darkest secrets has been well worth it.

I thank you for joining me on this journey of self-help and growth.

I thank you for taking the time out of your days and nights to learn about the story of a lost little boy who grew to be a positive difference maker — the story of a dreamer who never gave up on climbing out of the depths and touching the stars.

My Last Advice to You

My best advice to you, my friend, is to stay focused and have big dreams. Live in the here and now. The past brings back demons and the future is nothing without the present.

Travel, learn, love, grow, and live life to its very fullest.

We are all born with the potential for greatness. Never sell yourself short. Without big dreams, you have nothing to strive for. Find someone you can look up to — someone who can help you grow as a person.

Life is nothing more than a beautiful journey of self-discovery. Those of us who realize this will be the ones who own our destiny.

Live well. Do good deeds. Continue on your amazing journey of self-growth.

Make others smile and leave a lasting, positive impression in each person's mind. You never know who might make a great impact on your life, or you on theirs.

Treat everyone with the same love and respect that you feel you deserve. I do not care if you are a surgeon or a person walking on the side of the road, you still deserve my respect until you prove otherwise.

Put your heart into all that you do. People will take notice and aid you on your journey.

There's nothing better than hearing someone's beautiful discovery of inner growth.

Life is not about where you start. It is about the incredible journey you lead and what impact you make on others.

Thank you for reliving my life with me. I shed tears, cracked smiles, shook my head in disgust, and ended up thankful for each and every one of you.

I have so much more to share.

Until next time.

Thank You,

Jimmy "POP" Colson

ABOUT THE AUTHOR

Jimmy Colson

A husband and father, successful entrepreneur, bestselling author, marine life enthusiast, and motivational speaker, Jimmy Colson is on a mission to help change the world for the better, one person at a time.

Jimmy knows firsthand what it takes to grow a successful business from nothing. Homeless and living on the streets in Las Vegas, he now owns one of the fastest-growing orthotics and prosthetics companies in Las Vegas with three locations and more than 30 employees.

Precision Orthotics and Prosthetics (POP) is Jimmy's family-owned company with decades of experience in the fabrication and fitting of custom prosthetics and orthotics.

POP cares deeply about their patients and the community, donating shoes, bracing, and mastectomy products to local homeless and international missions every year as well as supporting many cancer foundations.

Jimmy is committed to giving back and helping others have a better life and greater chance to transform for the better. He has even received Congressional recognition for his good works in the community.

From the depths, Jimmy is on the rise! And he wants to help others rise too.

Jimmy and his wife Sara have much more planned to continue this mission!

Fun Fact:
Jimmy has had appearances on several TV shows including *Las Vegas Inked*, *Mad Hatters Tea Party* on the Food Network, four episodes of *Tanked* on Animal Planet, and *Lucky Chances* a mini-series with Jackie Collins.

WANT MORE?

Get in Touch

If you were inspired by Jimmy's journey, his stories, and his lessons learned, please reach out.

Jimmy is available for speaking engagements in the Las Vegas area, around the United States, and abroad.

Personal Website:
https://www.JimmyColson.com

Business Website:
https://www.ProstheticsLasVegas.com

Email:
info@JimmyColson.com

Published in partnership with
www.CopyThatPops.com

Made in the USA
San Bernardino, CA
14 January 2019